FROM BANKRUPTSY TO A MILLIONAIRE TWICE: A TRUE STORY

FROM BANKRUPTSY TO A MILLIONAIRE TWICE: A TRUE STORY

RON SEARCY

iUniverse LLC
Bloomington

FROM BANKRUPTSY TO A MILLIONAIRE - TWICE: A TRUE STORY

iUniverse books may be ordered through booksellers or by contacting:

iUniverse LLC
1663 Liberty Drive
Bloomington, IN 47403
www.iuniverse.com
1-800-Authors (1-800-288-4677)

ISBN: 978-1-4917-2976-2 (sc)
ISBN: 978-1-4917-2977-9 (e)

Printed in the United States of America.

iUniverse rev. date: 04/25/2014

MEMORIAL

To my daughter, Rhonda Lynn Sims Searcy. June 14th, 1974-April 11th, 2013. Daddy's Tooter Toots.

DEDICATION

I dedicate this book to the millions of people who just want a chance to show what they can do but, corporate America won't give them a chance. I want those of you that their inside is burning to make something out of their lives and be somebody, to know I did it and thousands of others without a degree have done it. You can because it's something you learn how to do plus your unbelievable desire to succeed, you can do it.

CONTENTS

PREFACE

There are millions of people living in a free enterprise system throughout the world that, are not doing anything with their life because our system pushes people down instead of, pushing people up.

I wrote this book about things that, I went through in my life and overcame many things that would have destroyed others. I was able to do so, simply because years ago, I read a book that absolutely changed my life.

I am in hopes that, after reading my book, you will realize that, for the most part, education and by education, I mean a college education, has absolutely nothing to do with obtaining wealth.

Early in my life I was physically abused, sexually abused, did not do well in school and was left thinking that, after graduation from high school, I was doomed to be a nobody.

Nine years after reading that book, I became a self-made millionaire, lost all of it and it took me another ten years to gain it all back. While having to deal with some health issues, all I had was stolen from me and I lost it all again.

By reading this book, I hope that it will inspire you and will also, open your eyes to the vast opportunities that are available to people that live in a free enterprise system and also realize that, the only thing keeping you from obtaining wealth is you.

CHAPTER 1

My Early Years

I was born in a small southern middle Tennessee town. My parents were raised on a farm but, worked all their lives in a factory. For the first twelve years of my life, my mom and dad rented from someone and when, I was about twelve years old, they were able, because of my mother, to purchase a home that, was about four miles further west from our previous home.

My father has been deceased a little over twenty five years and my mother is 90 years old as I write this book in 2007. I have two sisters. My oldest sister died, unexpected, in 2004. My youngest sister is ten years younger.

My mother is the most loving, caring and considerate person that, you would every want to meet and not because so much that, she is my mother but, because how she has lived her life in front of others. I have often said that if, my mother doesn't make it to heaven, the rest of us do not have a chance. Yes, she is a Christian woman.

I have no doubt that my father intended to be a good person and as far as lying, stealing, cheating or treating others bad, he was not guilty of any of the above however, he did have an extreme bad temper and as to me, he was very physically and mentally abusive.

I suppose that probably, the reason that I felt worthless and useless, stupid and dumb most of my pre-adult life had a great deal to do with him. For instance, he would try to help me with my homework and when I could not get a certain problem he would blow up on me and call me stupid and dumb, get up and leave. As I attended grammar school and even into high school I barely got by, making very low grades in most subjects. Actually, I hated school. I loved playing outdoors and spent a great deal of time out in the woods and up and down a creek that was nearby in order to stay away from him. My oldest sister was also very abusive to me. She would cause fights and was always bigger than me so, I got the raw end of the deal if, we fought. She would use her nails to scratch me up and I could see the pleasure she got from it on her face. She would also tell my dad lies to get me in trouble with him. I will admit that, I was bad about leaving my Dad's tools out and could not remember where I left them. I got many whippings from him over that one thing. I remember one night he came in from work (he worked the 2 PM to10 PM shift) and came to my room and jerked me out of the bed and started beating on me and telling me that, he told me to tie the dog. I kept telling him the dog was tied and we went outside after my beating and there the dog lay with the chain to his collar and how he missed the dog at the back of the garage I will never know because he had to drive straight up the drive with his head lights shinning right on the dog. The thing that stuck in my mind was he never apologized at all.

Another time, I had built a playhouse and my older sister was trying to get in my playhouse and I was hitting at her trying to keep her out and she had a popsicle which, was the old kind you freeze in the refrigerator in a little metal cup and put a stick for a handle to hold it and I accidentally knocked the popsicle off of the stick, hitting at her to keep her from getting in and she told my dad and my dad beat me until my back looked liked a black man yet, I am white.

Also I recall, on many occasions, my mother begging my dad to stop because, once he started spanking me, he did not know when to stop. Yet, another time, my dad lost his hair comb and blamed me for it and I got a spanking every morning for over three weeks until the comb was found. One day after getting my daily spanking, I went into the utility room to cry and just happened to notice the comb sticking out in the back pocket of his coveralls where he left it. Again, I never received an apology for that.

I recall very plainly that, until I got married at the age of nineteen (19), I literally hated my dad. His abuse made me feel unloved and unwanted. I do not recall my father ever telling me that, he loved me.

I realized, once that I matured that my dad really did love me and my disgust for him slowly went away after realizing that he really did not mean to be abusive because, otherwise, he was basically a good man so, I was able to forgive him.

When I got out of Grammar school, I had to go from a country school to the high school located in the county seat and again, because I did not make very good grades and the other classmates found out about it, I was made fun of and ridiculed. This, of course, did not help my self-esteem at all.

When I was a sophomore, my english teacher made fun of me in front of the whole class and embarrassed me so much that, I went to a study hall instead and as the principal told me at my graduating year that, I had the distinction of being the only person in the state of Tennessee that took freshman english, junior english, senior english and had to go back to summer school in order to take sophomore english.

After my parents bought the house when I was age twelve, there was a country store about one hundred fifty (150) yards east of our home and soon after we moved, this gentleman built a café onto the store. At that time, he put in pinball machines in the old store part and other gambling devices and did not carry as many grocery items. I went to work for him on a part-time basis and during this time period, he sexually abused me over about a two (2) year period. Now, this is one of those men that was in the church building every time the doors opened.

I might mention that, my father was a very negative-thinking person and was frightened to take any risks whatsoever. I told you this because, to my knowledge, my father never put one penny towards the payment of the home and my mother paid for it through blood, sweat, and tears.

I supposed that my father was what women in this day in time would call a 'control freak'. It definitely was his way or the highway. For instance, though my father allowed me to go to church with a neighbor each Sunday, he would not allow my mother to go because, he did not like her particular religious group.

Early in their marriage, my mother did know how to drive at one point, but in later years, she did not drive and soon forgot how to. My mother is probably one of the most uncoordinated people that you've ever meet in your life and that is the main reason why, I did not teach her how to drive after my father died even though, his car was still there. She got into the car to try and freshen her memory and backed over a swing set. That was the end of her driving. We finally sold the car.

When I was a little boy, around five (5) to seven (7) years old, I started attending church services and Sunday school. No one made me attend, I was just always drawn to God. My mom hadn't attended church for years because my dad wouldn't allow her to do so. Mom was very in subjection of my dad. She did start back a few years later.

You may not believe in God. You have that freedom in America. To me, I am in a win, win situation because, when all is said and done, I have nothing to lose. In fact, I have all to gain by being a student of the bible. God or, no God, by following the bible's teaching, it has made me a better person, a better father because it teaches one how to raise your children and teaches men to be a better husband and women how to be a better wife. I have often said that if the husband is following New Testament teaching about how a husband is to treat his wife and if the wife is also doing the things the bible teaches about being a good wife, it is impossible to ever get a divorce. Non believers have all to lose if they are wrong.

As you read this book, you will see how God brought me back to him when I failed to do his will and how he blessed me when I did, along with the punishment I received for turning my back on him.

I was attending a Baptist church with the people that mom and dad used to rent from but, one Sunday, the preacher tried to make me sit on the front two rows and that did not go over well with me so, I decided to go across the street to another congregation and at that time, I was around fourteen years old and was beginning to notice girls and I had seen three or four very good looking girls at the other church across the street so, this was not a hard decision for me.

I eventually dated three out of the four and now know that I probably could have dated the other one but, I thought she was so beautiful and was intimidated by her.

During the early years of my life, we lived in the country and so, at that time, we did not have television until, I was about ten or eleven years old and then, it was only black and white. In fact, for many years, we did not even have electricity so, we did our homework using lanterns and our heat was supplied by what we called an old Franklin heater that burned coal.

Each day when, I came home from school, the first thing I had to do was, to help wash dishes, along with my oldest sister. On Saturday, we had to dust and sweep the house and had other chores. I also had daily chores of going to the chicken house and gathering eggs and if, the coal supply got low, I had to bring in buckets of coal and in order to start a fire in the stove, we kept wood that had to be split. Also, Saturday was my mother's washing day and she would wash with a old timey ringer-type washer and a scrubbing board so, she had two large tubs that I had to fill with water that, we got from a well so, I had to draw the water from the well, fill the buckets, then, tote them around the house and I recall that, it took both of my hands to carry the water because I wasn't strong enough to carry two buckets at a time.

My father worked in a factory and he worked the 2 P.M. until 10 P.M. shift so, every evening, it was just me, my mother and my sister. My youngest sister wasn't born until I was age 10. We had to try to do our homework before it go too dark and if, we waited too late we had to use a kerosene lantern to work by.

I suppose I had a death wish when I was a small boy through my teen years. Actually, most was just plain stupidity. After my dad went to work at 2 PM, my sister, Elaine and I would beg mom to let us go swimming. My dad wouldn't let us do anything like that but, mom was a soft heart until we made her mad then, she would get a peach tree limb or, hackberry tree limb and wear out legs out. One day when I was about nine years old, we begged mom to let us go swimming in a nearby creek. I dove in, trying to impress my sister and dove straight into a big rock I couldn't see from the bank. I made a big gap in my head and it's a wonder I didn't get killed.

Then, there was the time my best friend, Woody and I built a five (5) story tree house in a triangle between three (3) trees. Woody stole some chewing tobacco from his grandfather and one day, Woody was working on an uncle's farm and I went to the top of the tree house and was fooling with the tobacco and accidentally swallowed it and I got dizzy and fell out of the tree.

I fell out like a sky diver and still remember on the way down, I thought, "superman". Ha I don't' recall how I made it back home but, mom said I fell through the door and fell down. My dad was about to leave for work and after finding out why I fell out of the tree house said, "good enough for you." Needless to say, that broke me from trying chewing tobacco. Ha

One day in February, it was really cold and Woody and I were out in the woods playing and we were close to a farmers pond when Woody dared me to strip down naked and go swimming. Well, stupid and prideful me took him up on his dare and jumped in.

A couple of days later, I got pneumonia but, mom thought it was just a regular bad cold. Now, this was during the days that doctors came to one's home as, back then, most couples had only one car. I recall being so sick that it was misery for mom to even try to wash me. When Doctor Birch was finally called, he looked at mom and told her my temperature was one hundred five (105) and if it got to one hundred and six (106), I would probably die. I stayed in the hospital for two weeks recovering. To this day, I have scar tissue on my lungs that shows up when an x-ray is done.

When my parents bought their first and only home, it was a mile and a half past where my old school bus turned off the main highway. I was nearly finished with the seventh (7th) grade and wanted to finish grammar school where I had always attended so, from mid march to the end of that school year in mid June and all of grade eight (8) the next year, I rode my bicycle to that turn off. I had bought a three speed bicycle the previous summer from working for different farmers at five dollars ($5.00) a day. One day on my way home, a guy I knew pulled up beside me and while talking to me, told me to hook my left arm inside his window so, I wouldn't have to pedal my bike. He decided to have some fun at my expense and slowly got his car up to ninety (90) miles per hour with me sitting on the bike. It's a wonder I didn't get killed.

I graduated from high school, after going to summer school, in nineteen hundred and sixty three (1963) and was seventeen and one half (17 ½) years old at the time therefore, I could not get a job in a factory so, I went to work on my first job with my uncle shoeing Tennessee walking horses and we traveled around several states and this is how I met my first wife. For the purposes of this book, I will call her Rose.

I met her in a small west Tennessee town as, she was working at a restaurant where we ate at on a part time basis, after school and it was absolutely love at first sight the minute I saw her.

We went out a couple of times and I did not hear from her for quite some time but, to my surprise, she wrote me a letter, months later, telling me that, I was the only man that had ever treated her decent and that, she wanted to see me again and by this time I had began to work for the Samsanite Corp. and had to drive thirty (30) miles one way to work each day and on the weekends, I would come home, take a bath and drive to west Tennessee in order to see her and this was well before the interstate systems were built. This went on for several months and I popped the, will you marry me question and we married in July of 1965.

I brought her to my mom's about thirty (30) days before we were married in order for her to have time to get a job because, I knew that I could not support both of us on the fifty six dollars ($56.00) a week I was making at that time. She got a job as a sales rep with a major department store but even with that, we still barely got by because hers was a part time job. I very well recall the first apartment we rented because it got so cold that first winter that, the water froze in the commode and this is in spite of having three (3) wall heaters in a one bedroom apartment going on high.

If, I recall correctly, she went to work for a pencil factory in nineteen hundred and sixty seven (1967) and later that year, I quit my job with the Samsanite Corp. and also went to work at the same factory. I was trained on a machine that, only two people in the USA knew how to run at that time and in February of nineteen hundred and sixty eight (1968), I received my draft notice to go to the Army and of course, this was during the Vietnam War period. I was smart enough to know that, if I allowed myself to be drafted that more than likely, I would end up in combat so, I signed up for an extra year in order to get a missile school that, was about fifty six (56) miles south from where I lived.

When I went to basic training at Ft. Campbell, Kentucky, my wife nearly had a nervous breakdown because, she had never been away from me and had told me that she had never dreamed that she would find a man that would treat her as good as I did. I was lucky enough to be stationed close to home for almost two (2) years

I started out taking a course in a missile launcher program which, was a fourteen week course and after about the eighth week, my instructor called me outside and told me that my grades had fallen below 75 and wanted to know if I was going to make it. I replied that, all the other guys are out every night chasing women but, that I was married and I spent all of my time studying but I could not seem to get electronics.

If, a student flunked out of the school that they signed up for, they had an automatic ticket to ammo humper's school which, basically means that they would carry ammunition packs out in the combat field and/or load and unload ammunition from cargo planes.

I cannot tell you the sick feeling that, I had walking from the school back to the company headquarters thinking that I was on my way to Vietnam combat. I stopped in the company headquarters and talked to my first sergeant and during the discussion, he found out that I knew how to swing a hammer and a little bit about carpentry work and he asked me if, I could fix some picnic tables that they had gotten torn up and he wanted those fixed so the students would have a place to get together after school. As we were walking down the side walk, on the way back, the first sergeant which, was an E-8 and I was a lowly private E-1, put his arm around me and said, "Searcy, being in the army, me and my wife move around a whole lot and don't have a whole lot of friends so, how about you and your wife come over for a visit this weekend"? I can tell you that the feeling I had at that moment was, like when, as a child, you get up and find out that Santa Claus has come. We became good friends and even though I did not know how to type, he put me in a position with that company as supply clerk and I had to hunt and peck but, I did the job and figured that was much better than going to Vietnam. After the minimum four (4) months in the Army, I received an automatic promotion to private E-2 and then after six (6) months, I was promoted to private E-3 and at that time, the company thought so much of me that they gave me a company order that made me an acting corporal or in other words, I had the authority but did not have the pay and once I did make corporal, in the 8th month, they issued a company order again that made me an acting sergeant where again, I had the authority but, did not the pay but, I was promoted to sergeant in the minimum of fifteen (15) months that was required because, after being supply clerk for a couple of months, the company commander from next door came over and was talking to the sergeant that was over me and kept looking in my direction and after this happened two or three times, I asked my sergeant what was going on and he let me know that the commander next door was losing his sergeant and that he was wanting me to come over and be his supply sergeant. My sergeant explained that would probably be the only way that I would get promoted since, there is only one slot in the present company that I was in for a supply sergeant so, I moved next door and found that there were no clothing records that, everything was in absolute disarray so, again, me being married, I did not believe in being unfaithful so, I spent all of my time between ninety (90) and one hundred (100) hours a week getting that place ready for a commanding general inspection. Once the inspection was made, I found out that I made a higher score than my former sergeant next door made on his even though he had been in the Army for nineteen (19) years. In addition, when I took over, the company commander was one thousand nine hundred ($1900.00) short on inventory of bedding and other supplies so, the first thing that I did was to make an inventory of all equipment and went all over that post, horse trading extra beds and lockers that I had for extra blankets and sheets and other things and I made up all of the shortages which, comes under the company commander which is personally responsible for and was thinking that he was going to have to pay this out of his own pocket but, because of my horse trading, he did not have to pay out anything so, after that, and along with my score on the commanding general inspection, this company commander thought that I hung the moon. I very often would ask for a three (3) day pass since, my home was such a short distance away and would get Friday, Saturday and Sunday off.

I did have an opportunity to go to Germany but decided that, they were going to leave me there until the rest of my time was up because, I had already gotten down to eleven (11) months remaining and I knew that Vietnam was twelve (12) months and Korea was thirteen (13) months but, that backfired on me as I got orders to go to South Korea. Then, after I left, my wife began to have problems again and I was able to get released from the Army a few months early in August of 1970.

CHAPTER 2

How I Got Started

After I got out of the army, I went to work for a local construction company, building homes.

This was in late August of 1970. I worked there until November of 1970 and was laid off because of the weather. In that particular region of the country, there is little to no home building being done during the winter months.

One day at lunch, another worker asked me what I was going to do and I told him I did not know but, I had a family to support and I had to do something. He suggested that we go to Chattanooga, Tennessee and I questioned what was available in Chattanooga and he said there was always a lot of construction going on there.

Sort of by blind faith, I decided to go with him and we stopped at my aunt's house and used her telephone and phone book and started calling contractors.

After making several calls, I made contact with a construction company that did only restoration work on home owner's insurance claims. This was all new to me because, at that time, I had always lived in the country and any home that I had ever seen catch fire, burned to the ground. So, I had no idea that there was a contracted that did this type of work.

We picked up another gentleman as a partner and the three of us would subcontract work from this contractor. At this time, all of us were as broke as one could be. We went without food for several days and I slept in the back seat of my car and also slept on a cot in one of the burned out houses.

About the same time, my oldest older sister called and said that my brother-in-law had gotten me a job with the company he worked for as an electrician's helper, starting at three dollars and twenty five cents ($3.25) an hour. Now, you will have to understand at that time, to me, that was rich because the going rate on most jobs was two dollars ($2.00) an hour.

I told my wife to call my sister and tell her that I appreciated what my brother-in-law had done but, I was going to keep working in Chattanooga. I also had withheld from my wife, until I got home, the fact that my first draw check worked out to be making over one hundred ($100.00) per day and I told her that I believed that there was more of that to be had.

I was in Chattanooga working on my birthday in December of 1970 and that day wound up being one of the low points in my life. After the three of us ended work, they asked me if I was going to do anything to celebrate my birthday and I stated that it wasn't a real big deal to me, just another day. Well, they stayed after me about going and having a couple of beers and shooting a couple of games of pool. I told them I was a married man and had no business in a bar. They came back with, we will just go shoot some pool, have a couple of beers, and come back early.

After the fifth time, I became convinced that there could be no harm in just shooting a couple of games of pool and having a couple of beers, so I agreed to go. That became one of the biggest mistakes I ever made in my life. They were correct except for one thing, the two beers turned into four or five beers and "Mrs. Wonderful" was sitting at the bar all by herself all decked out, very pretty, very sexy and very drunk. No, I did not hit on her as I was very happy at home and loved my wife very much but, she came over to the pool table under the pretense of me teaching her how to play pool, since I was very good at it. The more she rubbed around on me, touched me with her hands, the greater my lust became and so, before I knew what happened, I was in her car with her driving down a one way street the wrong way and going very fast in a small car. I was frightened out of my mind.

I have heard of many stories of people who commit fornication against their mate and in most cases, the guilty party is always sorry that they got caught, not truly sorry for the act . . . In my case, that is far from what happened. Immediately after having sex with this woman, I became so sick at my stomach because I let this woman tempt me into breaking an oath I made to myself when I got married.

Yes, she did forgive me and we remained married another nineteen (19) years but to this day, that still bothers my pride that I allowed that to happen. I hated myself and will never forget that lesson.

Just after this happened, one of my partners was always leaving the job and going for material at the lumber company and would stay gone two (2) to four (4) hours; leaving me and the other partner there to work. We finally found out that he was getting very small jobs and doing them by himself and still drawing a third (1/3) of what we were making on the burned out house so, we eliminated him.

A few weeks later, I got a phone call from the contractor at home. I had brought my wife to Chattanooga and rented a home there. The contractor stated that he was impressed by me and wanted to know if I would be interested in working for him as an estimator and he would train me in what I needed to know. I was fed up with the one partner left but I needed his knowledge to keep on doing the construction work so, I saw my chance to better myself and to get away from the other partner.

One of the lessons I learned is making a partnership work is even harder than making a marriage work.

During the time that I worked for the contractor as an estimator, my wife and I were on a visit on weekend to her brother and mother who lived in Northeast Arkansas. I also had an aunt on my mother's side and uncle who lived about thirty (30) miles away. They did not have any children and thought of me and my wife sort of as their children so; we would go see them when we made our trips to Arkansas.

We were very close to this aunt and uncle, as this uncle had Baptized my wife and I three or four years after we married.

During this particular time frame, we made a trip to Jonesboro, Arkansas to visit my aunt and uncle. My uncle had gone to make some cosmetic deliveries and my aunt and wife had gone to do some shopping and I was left alone in the house, and I am not speaking of hearing a voice, but something told me to get into the car and go to the mall.

Now, when you consider that I never go to the mall and that I had never been in a bookstore in my life, never heard of a motivational speaker and had never heard of a man named Zig Ziglar plus, I did not particularly like to read books then, you can see how this is very odd. I went to the mall and when straight to the bookstore, straight down the aisle to this book by Mr. Ziglar and the title of it was, "See You at the Top".

I could not put the book down. Mostly, it dealt was good old common sense reasoning. He reasoned that in a free enterprise system anyone could become a millionaire, and the only thing stopping them was the person. The book also gave me complete and total self-confidence. Add that to the fact I am a super competitive person and love to play card games, pool and board games and if, you play with me, I am going to try to kick your rear because I assume you are going to try and kick mine.

Shortly afterward, the contractor that I was working for sold his business to another gentleman and moved to San Diego. The new owner wanted to run the business himself, so I was out of a job. I guess you might say that I was forced to go into business for myself, however it wasn't quite as easy as I had pictured in my mind. You see, I had assumed that some of the insurance adjusters that I had been working with would give me a try, but I soon found out they would not.

We had moved to a duplex in another section of Chattanooga at this time and even though my wife connected with some home builders and was cleaning homes in preparation of the sale, we still just about starved to death. I remember endless days were we played card games and board games and basically sat around feeling sorry for ourselves and waiting for the phone to ring because I had ran an ad in one of those community shopper papers but, little by little I was able to pull us out of that and still maintain our credit. Also during this time, I was continuing to solicit business from insurance adjusters and by 1973, we bought a house in another section of town and my financial condition had improved tremendously.

I had around eight (8) men working for me and had also been able to purchase a couple of new pick up trucks and a new car.

My business was growing tremendously but, I did not have the operating capital that I needed so, one weekend when we had gone to visit my mother, I asked her if she would put a lien on her home and loan me five thousand dollars ($5,000.00). My father was not much of a business man and this request caused him to panic and unknown to anyone, he got up in the middle of the night and went into town and woke my older sister up and told her that they were going to lose their home if mom made that loan to me.

My wife was very good at doing hair though, she had not had any formal training and had previously agreed to fix my sister's hair the following morning and of course, not knowing my father had been there, walked into a hornet's nest so to speak.

My older sister(now deceased) jumped all over my wife about that.

When she returned to my mother's house and related all of this to me, I was so hurt and furious that I went on back home that day instead of the next day as planned.

That ordeal drove me even harder to become successful and later that year, we went for a visit and my older sister and her husband were at the lake camping out and boating and my mother wanted to go over and have a cook out with them. I cannot tell you how much pleasure I got when I drove up and my sister got one look at my car and asked how in the world could I afford a car like that? I decided that since she really couldn't grasp what I was doing so I replied, "Well, I figured the worst thing that could happen, was that they would come and get it."

After I returned home, on the following Saturday, I was looking out of the picture window in our living room and this man drove in our drive way got out and was walking behind both my cars, trucks, and boat with a clipboard and was dressed in a three piece suit and he finally came to the door and when I answered the door, he pulls out his badge and announced that he was a collection agent for the IRS and wanted to ask me some questions. I panicked even though I knew that I had not cheated the IRS but I figured he wouldn't be there unless he thought I had. I thought at the beginning he was there about my income tax but I soon found out he wasn't.

After sitting down, he started asking me all kinds of financial questions about my bank account, vehicles and rental properties that I had acquired. I told him all of the information that he wanted and by then my curiosity was up to the point that I finally asked him what this was all about. He asked me if I had previously had a certain gentleman work for me as a painter and I replied that yes, I did but I had fired him. He then asked me about a certain street address where I had previously worked on this person's property and asked me if on a certain date had I loaned a ladder to this painter. I replied that yes I did because the painter's ladder was not long enough to reach to gable end and I had a ladder that would and that I would let him use this ladder. The IRS agent asked if I had a receipt from where I rented the ladder to the painter. I replied that I did not. The agent told me that in that case, I owed the Internal Revenue Service fourteen thousand one hundred forty three dollars and fifty two cents ($14,143.52) for matching withholding that I did not pay. I replied that the painter was a subcontractor and did the job for a certain contract amount.

The agent stated that when I loaned him a ladder without renting the ladder to him that my actions were in violation of Internal Revenue guidelines and as far as they were concerned, when I loaned him a ladder, that made him an hourly employee and that they had gone back three (3) years to calculate matching withholding. So, that was my first run in with the good old IRS.

Two years later, in 1975, I was audited by the IRS for the first time. My wife did all of our bookkeeping and had made a mistake and it wound up that I got a five thousand dollar ($5000.00) credit from that audit.

As I am writing this book in the year 2007, to date, I have been audited four (4) times by the Internal Revenue Service and also had another run in with them in regards to one of the men who worked for me besides the one that I just told you about.

I had always wanted to return to my home county, so in the spring of 1977, I drove there to look for land to build a future home on. My intent was to purchase about ninety (90) to one hundred (100) acres and get that paid for and then build my dream home on it. I contacted a local realtor who was a high school classmate and he told me about a certain property and also about another farm that was three hundred forty eight (348) acres. I looked at the first property and it wasn't anywhere close to what I was wanting so, the other property was close by and just out of curiosity, I decided to drive by and take a look. It had a country house and 40 acres on one side of the road and 308 acres on the other side. The large track had a creek running through it, gentle rolling pastures and a small wooded area and was one of the most beautiful sites I has ever seen. I went by the realtor's office and no one was in except the secretary so, I left them an offer and I really didn't give it anymore thought. In fact, my offer was so ridiculous that I didn't even tell my wife about it.

About a week or so later, one night, I got a call from one of the realtors at that office and he told me that I had just bought a farm.

This was my first experience in purchasing real estate using my terms. Little did I know that when I made the offer that the owner of the property ran a sheet metal shop and did not have time to see after the old family farm. He had leased the farm to a neighbor, but the neighbor was not taking care of the property as he agreed and the owner viewed the property as a headache and just wanted to be rid of it. My offer to him was one hundred twenty five thousand dollars ($125,000.00) for the property with fifteen thousand dollars ($15,000.00) down at seven percent (7%) interest and the owner carried the note, paid in annual payments of fourteen thousand dollars ($14,000.00) each.

It was somewhat difficult for my wife to leave a very nice home in Chattanooga and move to a farmhouse that needed a complete redoing but, we both wanted out of the rat race and so, we moved in June of 1977. It took me four (4) years part time to completely restore the home. I put a new roof, new siding, re-wired and re-plumbed the house and it was a doll house inside. I left the exterior looking like an original farm house.

At one point, I had one hundred ten (110) head of cattle, a huge hog operation and was absolutely living my dream.

After working on a farm for many years and hauling hay, fixing fences and other chores, I believe this was the only time I really enjoyed physical labor.

From 1977 to 1982, I was able to do quite a bit of insurance claims repair work in the area that I lived in, working twelve (12) men full time.

In 1980, a friend of mine at church lost his job as a mortgage processor because of the high interest rates and the fact that no homes were selling at that time. He had a wife and two (2) children and was in desperate need of a job and so, since he had construction background and knowledge, I opened a branch office in Nashville, Tennessee. I was busy working on the farm, hunting and fishing and wasn't paying enough attention to business as I should have.

I learned a hard lesson in that no one else is going to do things the way that you do them and though he worked hard, there is a lot more to that business than just working hard. For instance, the day doesn't just end at 5 PM like for everyone else. In order to keep the jobs running smoothly, they have to be coordinated which means, most of the subcontractors and workers cannot be reached until the evening hours and to delay the calling of different trades, is a major mistake in my business.

Once I realized that something was wrong, it was too late. I did take over the business a few months later and made a lot of money, however the interest rates were so high I couldn't make enough money to even pay the interest so; with most of my operating capital gone I was left with no choice but to file personal bankruptcy. I put this off for a couple of months because of my pride. I was raised to believe that you paid your bills and that anyone who filed bankruptcy was a deadbeat, crook or both.

Since then, I have learned to be a little less critical when I have to walk in someone else's shoes. I now understand that bad things can happen to good people that are beyond their control. Needless to say, I can't explain in words the feeling that I had because I absolutely loved that farm. I owned most of the land around me so, there was only one neighbor I could see and they were a retired couple and I could sit outside late in the afternoon with a cup of coffee and the only thing I could hear would be the birds singing and the creek running. There were no automobile, airplane or any other outside noise.

I waited too late in the year to auction the farm because property doesn't sell very well that time of year.

I had hoped to get enough from the auction to pay off all of the debts, but basically all I got is one of the worst sick feelings I have ever had in my life. For instance, cows that I gave six hundred dollars ($600.00) each for, sold for three hundred dollars ($300.00) to four hundred dollars ($400.00). A brand new air conditioned tractor that cost forty five thousand dollars ($45,000.00), sold for fifteen thousand dollars ($15,000.00) and those were just two small examples of how the auction went. I remember telling my wife that if crying would help any, I could fill a tub full.

The house did not auction for anything close to the market value was so, we remained at the house for a few months trying to sell it separately on the market.

The house finally sold and we moved to the city in a much larger home. I had a pickup truck and my wife had a 1983 Lincoln town car that was practically new however, the attorney who handled my bankruptcy advised me that I didn't have to make any payments and that the car was mine.

One morning, I got up and looked out of the window and found out that the advice my attorney gave me was not valid because, the repo-man came during the night and took the car. That was just as well because I couldn't afford the payments.

CHAPTER 3

Unexpected Divorce

After the auction of my farm, we remained at the farm house for a while and then we decided to move to the city and sell the farm house.

I had quit the construction business for lack of operating capital and one night I got a telephone call from an insurance adjuster friend of mine asking me if, I would like to come to work with him as insurance adjuster and so, I went to work for him for a few months. He was a jerk to work for and we parted company. My money soon ran out and I could not afford to pay rent any more. I suppose this was the lowest time in my life. I had to suck in my pride and move my family in with my mother.

This, I suppose, helped both of us since, my father was already deceased and my mother was living on social security, barely getting by.

During the time period that we lived with my mother, my wife and I both, got involved with a multi level company that taught people about basic financial planning and I cannot explain in words the worry and down and out feeling that I had for several years in trying to make that business work. My wife and I both absolutely worked our rear ends off but, we barely made enough to survive on and many times we did not even make that.

As I said before, my wife's mother and brother both lived in northeast Arkansas and so, in 1987 she asked me how I felt about moving there. She did know that I absolutely hated the place because of so many insects as, there was no such thing as standing around and talking on the outside during the summer months or getting a cup of coffee and sitting under a shade tree late in the afternoon because the mosquitoes would absolutely eat you alive. Also, the land there is flat as a pancake and all you see is soy beans and cotton with just a very few scattered trees where in middle Tennessee, I have always felt that it was one of the more beautiful places that I had ever seen, having traveled around half the world.

My ex-brother-in-law, Carl, was almost like a brother and I will say to anyone that he is one of the finest human beings that I have ever met. Not only did I consider him my brother-in-law, I considered him one of my best friends as he is one of few that never did mess over me.

In discussing the possibility of me coming to Arkansas, my brother-in-law realized that I would need some financial help and asked me about how much I would need. I told him probably about one thousand five hundred dollars ($1,500.00) so, when we got to Arkansas I tried to restart the construction business and needless to say, that takes a while of constant solicitation on my part before I finally get someone to give me a try.

Over the first few weeks, the bills kept piling up. We rented a house from my sister-in-law, Janet. I could not pay the rent so, I did some work on the house in exchange for the rent to begin with and my brother-in-law and my mother-in-law, Juanita were bringing some food to us but, they got very inpatient with me, and not understanding that it takes time for a person's efforts to pay off and when the amount that I owed my brother-in-law got up to one thousand four hundred dollars ($1,400.00), I think about everyone had given up on me except for myself.

One day, my brother-in-law and sister-in-law came by the house and my sister-in-law came by our house and expressed concern about me not working. The problem was not my willingness to work because very few people could outwork me physically, the problem was they were wanting me to get me a job in a factory but, that would not pay enough to make my bills therefore, I would go in a hole every month and I believed in myself enough that, I knew that my insurance claims repair business would get rolling, given time. It wasn't long after this that, I got my first job and did most of the work myself and repaid my brother-in-law in full.

We had been there only a few months when my brother-in-law's best friend which, was an acquaintance of my wife and myself for many years, separated from his wife and he wanted her back and he started back drinking and started back smoking and started hanging around us sort of crying in his beer so to speak. My brother-in-law lived about a one half mile down the road from us and we were always together watching movies, cooking out, playing cards or doing something together and so, this man started to hang out with us because we were all aquatinted, I thought nothing about him calling my house and talking to my wife on several occasions and also, when she took my daughter to school, she would go by his hardware store and they would go and have coffee and talk.

Now, for those who think like her, in Matthew chapter 5, verse 32, Jesus said that if a man looks on a woman, to lust after her, he has committed adultery in his mind already." First, Jesus knows the difference between the words, adultery and fornication. He didn't say fornication. The Greek word for fornication is a noun and is, "Meiches." That is not the word used here. The Greek word used here is, Meicheou, a verb that means, "Those who are drawn away by a Jezebels solicitations." So, you see, it doesn't mean every time any man lusts after a woman, he did the same thing as fornication. Come on, if that was true, no man would ever make it to heaven because every man has been guilty of that at one time or, another. Oh at the excuses people use for their sins.

My wife asked me for a divorce. She married the man who had hung around with us. He died of cancer in 2013 and my uncle had a stroke years ago and can't speak.

Having been married for twenty three (23) years at the time and never ever dreaming that, I would ever get a divorce, I was absolutely devastated because, I thought that, we were the all American couple. I suppose that, I will have to take at least part of the blame because, once we moved to Arkansas, I did not provide the spiritual leadership that I should have and stopped attending church services on a regular basis.

Like a fool, I rented an apartment about thirty (30) miles away from her home and did and said everything I knew to say and do to try to save our marriage but, I finally figured out that one person cannot save it by themselves and most importantly, no matter how good a person you are, if, the other person doesn't love you anymore, they just do not love you and there is nothing you can say or do to make them love you therefore, it is time to get on with your life.

On a visit to my apartment, my oldest daughter, Pamela, suggested that, I get back into the insurance claim repair business because, she said, no one was any better at it than I was so, I decided to go to back to Tennessee.

I found a motel room with a kitchenette and of course, I can now look back and laugh at it but, it wasn't very funny at the time because, I was very close to being homeless. I did not have any utensils so I purchased cans of food at the grocery store and would warm them on the stove eye and eat out of the can with a plastic spoon that I got from a local restaurant where I went to have coffee.

When I came back to Nashville, I had a total of four hundred dollars ($400.00) to my name and I went to a pawn shop and hocked the diamond ring and a deer rifle that, I thought the world of, but a person has to do what they have to do. I eventually got the ring back. I also bought another rifle.

I contacted several insurance companies that I had previously worked with and it wasn't long before I started to getting in some small jobs and so, I got out my paint brush and nail apron again and started to do the work myself until, I could hire a carpenter to help me and after a few weeks, I was able to hire a helper to work with him and I spent my time running their material for them to save myself money, pick up trash on jobs and also continued to solicit business. Within about three (3) month's time, I had made thirty thousand ($30,000.00).

I had always held the belief that, I never would move in a woman's home or have a woman move in with me if, I wasn't married to them but, I suppose the old saying goes "until you walk in someone else's shoes". I never knew that I was going to be that lonely and especially after being married that many years I wasn't use to the dating scene and it didn't take me very long to begin to absolutely hate it with people lying about what they look like and playing games with your mind so, I met this lady that I will call, Brenda that seemed extremely compatible to me and though I did care about her a lot, I never was in love with her. What I mean is, we both liked doing basically the same things and watching movies, fishing, gardening and playing different types of card and board games. I thought, hey, I could do worse. She was crazy about me. However, she was not only what I call insanely jealous, she became greedy about the money.

I began my relationship with this woman in January 1989 and after about a year, I did not have the money at that time to be able to go out on my own, as I had a couple of financial set backs and she gave me an ultimatum to either marry her or move out and so I had no choice but to marry her however, later I discovered that this lady did not have a scriptural divorce and if you read my first book, "Divorced at the court house but not in heaven", you will see why I left her.

In 1992, I got a call from an independent adjusting firm two (2) days after hurricane Andrew hit south Florida and was offered an opportunity to be guaranteed one thousand dollars ($1,000.00) a day to come work as an independent adjuster on commission basis and I just could not pass that up. I made a lot more than what I was guaranteed and was able to payoff all of my bills and have money left over. I cannot tell you the feeling that I had in early 1993 when drove off the car dealership parking lot in Hollywood, Florida with a brand new Lincoln Town Car.

You see, since my bankruptcy ten (10) years earlier, it had been nothing but an absolute nightmare because people viewed me as piece of trash whenever any creditor found out that I had filed bankruptcy. Also, I believe everyone in my family and all of my friends had given up on me but I never gave up on myself. I knew that I would be back but I just didn't know exactly how to go about doing it. The money that I made from working as an adjuster gave me the operating capital that I needed to get my construction business really going good so, after I returned home from working hurricane Andrew I restarted my construction business.

I left this woman in October of 1995 and in March of 1996, I met a woman that I will call, Jane that was fifteen (15) years younger than me and looked very close to what the late Marilyn Monroe looked like, including face and figure. Now, don't let your mind go to the gutter, I am not some dirty old man that was seeking a younger woman, it just happened that way and it never was an issue one way or another. In fact; I often teased her about not being able to keep up with me.

CHAPTER 4

Oh No, Not Again

In the spring of 1996, I had been on the dating scene for several months and was absolutely fed up with all the lies, cons, and game players and was to a point that I didn't even want to go out any longer. At one point, I was on a call in singles line and I met thirteen (13) out of thirteen (13) women who either lied about their weight or what they looked like. Most of them were seventy-five (75) pounds or more then they indicated and I soon found out that their definition of beautiful was far from mine.

One night, I was in a restaurant and in walked this gorgeous blond that looked very much like the late Marilyn Monroe and I later found out that she worked in cosmetics with a store that was close by and had come in to get a soft drink on the way home. I just had to meet her and I did get her telephone number at work but, I didn't hear from her for a couple of days so I called her work number and asked, "Have you divorced me already."

We made arrangements to have our first date the following Friday. I took her to one of the nicer restaurants in town and during dinner, she pressed her leg against mine under the table and I knew then that she liked me very much. I sure liked her because she was an absolute head turner and as time went on, every restaurant we went to, she turned every guys head when she walked into the room. Certainly, being a man it didn't hurt that she had a playboy figure to go along with her looks. From the very first, we just seemed to click and as I write this seventeen (17) years after meeting her, she is still my best friend and buddy though, we are not involved romantically. We talk all the time and eat out a lot and I think one of the main things that drew us together is the fact that we have so much fun together. Her mother can hear her laughing and know immediately who she is talking to on the phone.

While I was dating my soon to be, wife, Jane, which, was the summer of 1996, I received notice from the IRS that I owed them five thousand ($5,000.00) for a deduction I took in 1993 that, was taken on the apartment I had rented in Miami and due to the experiences that I had already had with the IRS, I thought, "Oh no, here we go again".

I made an appointment with one their representatives and went down to find out what this was all about and was told that since I spent a year in Miami that was my "tax home" and they were not going to allow the deduction I took for my apartment and utilities. This went on back and forth for several months and I finally realized that the IRS thought that I had done something wrong because, they not only where after me for that they decided to audit me for three (3) years back and when they did this, I realized they were flat after me, so I hired a CPA to take care of the matter for me.

I hope that what I am about to tell you will be some form of inspiration for you in dealing with problems in life because, my wife, Jane, while dating came by my apartment while I was on the phone to the IRS and later we had a very nice romantic dinner and she was amazed because it didn't seem to bother me and told me that if she had been told that she owed the IRS five thousand dollars ($5,000.00) she would be in a panic. I replied that the reason I handled it the way I did, I either owed them what they said I owed and if I did, I would pay them or I don't owe them which I won't have to pay anything or I don't owe as much as they say I owe them so since I do not know the answer yet there was no reason to be all upset.

After dating for several months, I asked her to marry me and we married in October of 1996 or should I say, I thought I was married. We had looked at a home and signed a contract to purchase the home, but it wasn't available for two (2) to three (3) weeks after we married so, I remained at the apartment I was at and she remained at her mother's along with her daughter. Her daughter was five (5) years old at the time.

About a week after we married I had lunch with her one day and as I checked my mail at the apartment, I saw a letter to me from the attorney's office that handled my last divorce. I was absolutely blown away when I opened the letter and found a note from the attorney apologizing for the delay in filing my divorce papers in a timely manner.

Back in July of that year, I was told when the court date would be and thirty (30) days after that date I would be a free man. I found out though that the attorney's secretary failed to file the proper paperwork when she was supposed to and that, when I married the last time, I was still married to my second wife. Yes, that made me a bigamist. Can you believe the messes I get into? How can someone trying to do so right get into all of this?

I panicked and called the district attorney in the county where the divorced was filed and to my surprise he more or less laughed at me saying, "Got yourself into a mess haven't you." He explained that since it was an honest mistake that he wouldn't pursue charges against me.

I then called the district attorney in my home county where I got the license and he basically got a good laugh out of it and

I suppose he could hear the desperation in my voice and he also told me that he wouldn't press charges against me and that all I had to do was obtain another license.

Well, I still wasn't sure, so I called another county district attorney where the marriage had actually taken place and basically got the same statement from the district attorney there.

This was too close to the holidays and knowing that my wife was going through a lot of stress from having to move back to her mom's house, right or wrong, I decided that I didn't want to mess up her holidays and I would wait until after the first of the year to tell her, fully intending to simply remarry her by obtaining a new license.

In November, we moved into the home. I did not intend to tell her about the marriage license mistake until after the first of the year, however on New Year's Eve of 1996, we went out to dinner and got into an argument and on the way home, I told her. Needless to say, it didn't go over very well at all.

During the time period we dated from April 1996 until we married in October of 1996, she never showed any indication at all of having a bad temper but, after we moved into the new house, it immediately came out.

I was able to use the money from hurricane Andrew to keep expanding my business and I finally reached a point that, I had several branch offices and was making what most people would consider mega bucks or in other words more than a quarter of a million dollars a year and not only was I able to purchase a home for me and my wife, I purchased new vehicles almost every year and was able to buy some rental property.

In my living room, I had a fire place opening and I am sure you have seen those openings where a piece of metal painted black is put into the opening to cover the hole and one day my wife was drawing a beautiful vase and a set of flowers that came out of the vase and I noticed that she did not have a magazine or book that she was looking at and I asked her if, she was drawing that from out of her head and she said that she was and I told her that, she had God given talent that is very exceptional.

I then told her a story about a time when I had my farm that I got some junk mail and the title of this book that this guy wanted me to order was, "$25,000.00 for a few hours work doesn't seem quite fair". I decided that, anyone that had a book titled like that was going to get my ten dollars ($10.00) because; I had to find out what he had to say. When I got the book, I found that, he was trying to convince the reader that, there were more new millionaires each year in the self publishing business in American than anything else and there was at least one good book in each individual. Also, he stated that if you did not know something to write a book about then pick a subject that you liked and go to the library and research enough books where you could write your own book. Now, this was a time before fax machines, computers and other methods that have now come about in the publishing and printing business and he was basically using mailing lists of people that had previously ordered his type of book and he had a very elaborate system where according to him, every time him he put it in place he would make over a million dollars.

In reading that book, my wife got the idea to do a children's book and she did her own illustrations and after she produced the book and of course, this is before it was actually printed, she took it to her daughter's school and all the kids went wild over it and so I asked her about a woman that she had mentioned that worked for a major publishing company and already published children books and she said that she use to go to church with that woman so, I suggested that she call the lady and have lunch with her.

After having her luncheon, she came back very excited and decided to go ahead and send her book to the Library of Congress for her copyright. She sort of put the book on the back burner because, I did not have the spare money, at that time, to pay for having her book published but, one day, she received a letter from a publisher that had found her book at the Library of Congress and sent her a contract for thirty percent (30%) which, is excellent in the publishing business.

For myself, during July of 1993 while I was in Miami working hurricane Andrew, one Sunday morning I was in my apartment by myself and I am not talking about hearing a literal voice but, something told me to get my bible and open it to Romans, Chapter 7, where it says, "the wife that has a husband is bound to her husband for as long as he shall live therefore, if she would be married to another while her husband is alive, she shall be called an adulteress". The same voice told me to turn to Matthew, Chapter 19, where Jesus gave the divorce law and it didn't take very long to dawn on me that the religious world had made a blunder in assuming that the divorce law that Jesus gave applied to both men and women but, it doesn't. The reason that it doesn't, is first, it is a historical fact that women up to the time that Jesus gave, that law women never had the right to divorce their husband. Secondly, when you understand who was present which, were men because women were not allowed in those discussions and also, what these men understood in their minds. They understood that they could get rid of their wife anytime they decided they wanted to by giving her a written document. Jesus put a screeching halt to that and told them the only way they could get rid of their wife is if she committed fornication or, in other words sexual infidelity and if they did do that and marry somebody else, they would be guilty of adultery and if someone married her that he had put away for the wrong reason would also commit adultery This is why I wrote and published the book "Divorced at the court house but not in heaven".

In the year 2000, I went for my annual physical and found out that I had an enlarged heart that was due to high blood pressure and high blood pressure was due from stress so, in other words, my business was going to put me in the grave if I kept on with the construction business. I didn't have to worry about getting out of that business as; you will soon read about how greed and unbelievable events put me out.

Now, back to what I was saying earlier about going to the doctor for an annual physical years ago. I have always had very good check-ups and there was never any problem and this time, I could tell from the look on the doctor's face that something was very wrong. After he told me about the high cholesterol and the high blood pressure, he gave me a prescription for medication. Over a two (2) year period, I kept telling him that something else is wrong because, I could not hardly get my breath at times, couldn't walk very far yet, I knew I didn't have emphysema from my smoking because of chest X-rays that had been done within this time frame. I also told him that sometimes when I lay down to take a nap or to go to sleep at night I would wake up feeling like someone had a pillow over my face, trying to smother me. I also explained to him that I had never had heart burn before and now everything that I ate caused me to have heart burn. He told me that I was just getting older. I was about age fifty three (53) at this time.

When I first went to him, I had told him that my father and his two (2) brothers all died of a heart attack due to blockage in their arteries and that I wanted tests done every time I had a physical. Evidently, this was never done.

After constantly complaining, my regular doctor finally sent me to a cardiologist that gave me a stress test and other tests and declared that I had a heart valve that wasn't opening and closing properly and that it was very common in my age range and that he would give me medication to take care of that. As you will see in a minute, not only did my regular doctor misdiagnose me, so did the cardiologist.

Also during this two (2) year time frame, I went to dinner one night and had a mixed drink called, a white Russian and after drinking one of them, my blood pressure went crazy and I wound up in the emergency room at the hospital and on the way there I was telling my wife what to take care of because it was so bad and I was in such pain and misery that I didn't think I would live to get to the hospital. Neither did she.

On another occasion, I was visiting one of my branch offices out of town and one morning when I got up, it was raining very hard so, I decided to have coffee in my room instead of going to a restaurant however, my doctor had taken me off of caffeinated coffee and I had been drinking decaffeinated for quite some time but, the motel only had caffeinated coffee so, I had two (2) cups and two (2) hours later, my blood pressure was going nuts again and I had to go to the hospital emergency room again.

A couple of months later, I was out for a romantic dinner again and again, not realizing what caused it, drank about a half of a glass of the same mixed drink and before dinner was over, my blood pressure went nuts again and this time, I told my wife to take me to a well known heart hospital emergency room and I wasn't there for more than twenty (20) minutes before this surgeon came in and explained to me that he had bad news and good news. I said, "Well, give me the good news first." He told me that the good news was that, I didn't have anything wrong with my heart but, the bad news was that I had been misdiagnosed for two years and that I now had ninety five percent (95%) blockage in my main artery and that I could die at any moment so, he was going to have to do emergency quadruple bypass heart surgery on me. I told him if that was the case then to get me to the operating room right then.

Needless to say, I survived the operation but, it took about five (5) months before I could really function properly and everything healed.

In the surgery, they cut my breastplate in order to make the incision for the operation and though I slept on a waterbed, I was so sore that I could not rest on the waterbed. It was also extremely painful for me to get into and out of the bed. The only way that I could sleep was in a lounge chair so, that is where I slept for five (5) to six (6) months. Even after that period of time, it was months before I could even take a shower because the water hitting my chest was extremely painful so I had to take a bath out of the sink using a wash rag.

During the two(2) years prior to my operation, I really had things going pretty good, having several branch offices of my business and my income for those two (2) years was three hundred twenty five thousand dollars ($325,000.00) and the year prior to my operation, I made three hundred fifty thousand dollars ($350,000.00). Not too bad for an old country boy with a high school education and with a sister who said I would never amount to anything.

Now for the bad news. What follows next is sort of like the old show on television several years ago that had this little song that said, "If I didn't have any bad luck then I wouldn't have any luck at all."

I had one gentleman at my home office that I guess, I always felt sorry for and even on the day that I met him and his son on an interview for them to be carpenters, I found out that they were religious men and were in very bad shape financially and on that very day I loaned each of them five thousand dollars ($5,000.00) Yes, I know that was a crazy thing to do. The son was almost as talented as his dad, having worked with his dad for many years although he was only twenty three (23) or twenty four (24) years old at the time I met him.

I put the son to work as a carpenter and hired a helper to work with him and the father, Ray, had estimating abilities although his experience was very limited but, I trained him to write estimates the way that I wanted them done. I suppose that, in the back of my mind, I always knew that he had the talent and the ability, he did not seem to follow instructions very well nor did he have very much ambition and I should have fired him many times but I did not. He constantly caused me to lose money on jobs because of improper estimating and/or running the jobs. I had a man running the office in Knoxville, TN who had been a close personal friend of mine for twenty years. I had another guy in Madisonville, KY that had become a fairly close friend and, I had known him when he was an insurance adjustor and had worked several claims with him before I had hired him to work for me. At the time I did hire him, he too was in dire financial stress, being behind on his child support payments with an ex-wife threatening to put him in jail so, I loaned him five thousand dollars ($5000). I did get all of this money from all individuals paid back to me however, you will see in a minute how they all turned on me. Again, I had another gentleman in Shelbyville, TN that was the best estimator and branch manager that I had though, he was somewhat cocky, and he was a very good estimator and did an excellent job of running the jobs and collecting my money. Here is how my world fell apart in a matter of months.

One estimator had two jobs that, back to back, I lost over ten thousand ($10,000.00) on each job because he wasn't watching the subcontractors and checking the quality of their work and I had to go back and redo almost everything that had been done in order to maintain the quality that was expected. The gentleman in Shelbyville, TN was working with one adjustor however this one adjustor gave him so much business that he made me over one hundred thousand dollars ($100,000.00) a year. I tried and tried to get him to solicit business and in fact, I tried to get all the branch managers to solicit business but, I couldn't make them because they were on a commission basis and to force them to do that would be against Internal Revenue guidelines as to whether someone is an hourly employee or a subcontractor.

Even though the contract had certain guidelines, under Internal Revenue guidelines, I cannot tell a subcontractor or someone on commission what time to start work, what time to quit, or manage them in any way, as to how they go about doing their job.

I might mention that all the things that are to follow here, happened during a one (1) to two (2) year period and are not necessarily in chronological order.

In April of 1998 a tornado hit a section of Nashville, Tennessee and I was absolutely swamped with work. I worked seventeen (17) hours a day, seven (7) days a week for several months, trying to keep up with all the claims that were coming in. I also brought workers in from branch offices that were close by and I also hired several roofing crews but, still could not keep up with all the work. It was almost a year before all the roofs and structural damage was repaired even though, I had dozens of men working on these claims. Of course, I also had my regular business and had five (5) or six (6) house fires and other minor claims that, my regular crews were working on.

In 1990 I had met an older gentleman who had a lifetime of being in the construction business, doing commercial work and building homes. This gentleman was in the home building business but, later switched to commercial drywall work. Though I would see him from time to time, it had been approximately two (2) years since, I had last contact with him prior to the tornado.

After I received the book, "$25,000 for a few hours work didn't seem quite fair," I sat down and wrote an insurance claims repair manual in 1983. I had given Tom a copy of this manual back in 1990 because, that was the period of time that, I was sort of 'down and out' and got the idea of finding contractors that, were already in the construction business and agreeing to teach them the insurance claims repair business. I got ten percent (10%) of their gross sales in return for my knowledge.

I contacted him just prior to the tornado to see if, he had a copy because I did not have the manual on computer at that time and had misplaced my copy so, I wanted to use his copy to make one for myself.

He explained to me that he had gotten into financial trouble and was having to file bankruptcy and was looking for a job so, after one(1) or two (2) meetings, I decided to hire him.

Over the years, I have learned sadly, that when someone goes around talking about Jesus all the time, I had better watch out. This is not true of everyone, of course, but it sure wound up that way with him as, you will see.

We agreed on a five hundred dollar ($500.00) per week draw against commission and right away, he seemed very aggressive and within the first month, he got me three (3) new accounts. Two (2) of those accounts did not produce very much business but, one (1) account just absolutely poured the business on me, during the time of the tornado of 1998.

In the contract, in order to earn his commission, there were three things that were required of him. All of my contracts with my branch managers and my contractors in the home office were the same. Those three things were: (1) he was to estimate the job which means, he goes out to the job site and makes a list of the damages either on a tape recorder or are hand written. To do this properly (the way insurance adjusters want it), it is done room-by-room, item-by-item in that particular room without skipping around from one place to another. Then, it also included putting the estimates into an estimating program that, I had on the computer. All of my branch managers had fax machines and computers and everyone in the home office had a computer except for the new personnel which, he was. To give him plenty of time to get this done, I had two (2) computers in my office. (2) The second thing that he was to do was, to run the jobs. This means that, he is to schedule and coordinate all workers and sub-contractors, to make sure that the job goes in a timely manner. He was to oversee the entire job until, it was finished. (3) The third thing, he was to do was, to collect the money from the jobs once they were completed.

It seemed that he got in his head to go out to a job and do a scope equaled ten (10) percent. During about a six (6) to eight (8) week period of working for me, he only ran three (3) or four (4) jobs and did a poor job of overseeing that work. On two (2) of the fire jobs, I had to have other crews go in and redo the work because, he failed to check out the sub-contractors that he hired.

In order to get his jobs out, I had to solicit the help of another estimator and let him help schedule the work on some of Tom's jobs. Tom also would not follow instructions and would bring in a bunch of scribbled notes that no one could tell what he was figuring.

Actually, some of the other estimators saw the older gentleman's scope and said it looked like a chicken scratching because he skipped around and just had notes all over the page.

I tried several times, unsuccessfully, to teach him how to operate the computer estimating system but, maybe because he was sixty six (66) and was stuck in his ways, he just could not learn the system and I was just so busy that I didn't have time to fool with him anymore so, I stayed up late and got up early and ran his estimates for him. So here again, he did not do all that was required under his contract. In addition, he did not ever collect one penny on any of his jobs.

From the very beginning, Tom attempted to change the way my company was run and though, I certainly was always open for suggestions on anything I thought would make things better, it was almost a daily thing with him. I also found out that he was sowing discord among the other workers and even planned on going on his own but, he knew that he did not know enough about the insurance claims repair business so, he asked another estimator about going in with him.

When that information was brought to my attention, I had no choice but to fire him rather than sit back and watch him slowly but surely destroy my company by sowing discord among the others.

I might mention that, prior to any association with him; he had been in several lawsuits with others that he disagreed with.

After firing him, I sent him a letter asking him to return all of my forms and equipment that had been furnished to him as the contract required return of all these items.

He did return all the equipment, however he kept all copies of all estimates he had along with copies of all my contracts and other forms that I used.

If, I recall correctly, he sent a list of jobs that he felt I still I owed him money on that totaled over thirty thousand dollars ($30,000.00). I wrote to him and explained what the contract called for and because he did not do the items required under our contract I did not owe him anything at all. During a six (6) week period that he worked, he was paid over sixteen thousand dollars ($16,000.00).

He complained to the general contractors' licensing board with the state and after receiving my response to his complaint, the license board sent a letter to him and sent me a copy that said, this complaint did not have any merit.

He then hired an attorney and after contacting his attorney, I made him aware that the contract called for binding arbitration in the event we had any disagreements. The attorney asked me if I cared who the umpire was and believing that any umpire would be a fool to award him anything since it was clear that he did not do the requirements under our contract so, I agreed to let his attorney pick the umpire. This was a major miscalculation on my part. I also know better than to go into court or any arbitration hearing without an attorney to represent me however, due to the circumstances of him not doing what the contract called for, I did not feel that I needed one. Yes, you guessed it, I lost.

I got a real good education about binding arbitration. I found out that once a ruling is made and a ruling is recorded, it is almost impossible to overturn an arbitration case. I did appeal however, on an appeal; they will not rehear the case again. I had to prove either miscalculation of figures or fraud.

Something that is quite interesting that I found out later is the umpire was not only a former judge that his attorney had cases before him; he was also the uncle of Jane's ex-husband. I found it very hard to believe when he testified that he did not recognize my last name. Anyhow, as the saying goes, it is one thing to win a lawsuit against someone it is another thing to collect the money so, I have not paid one penny since he won the arbitration case 1998 and it is now 2013 nor do I ever intend to pay him anything. To me right is right and wrong is wrong and I will not be done wrong.

In addition to all of this involvement with him, shortly after I fired him, I took over the jobs that he had going at that time and on one job, the homeowner was very difficult to deal with in the beginning and because some of these jobs took so long, this homeowner called one day and wanted out of his contract. We had completed all exterior work so I told him I would make a list of all items not done because I felt it was easy to put that list together since all interior work had not been done so, I did this and mailed it to him. He called me back about a couple items on the exterior that was not done so, I agreed on those items and sent him a check and thought that it was over however, I found out that he had not cashed either check, which totaled almost ten thousand dollars ($10,000.00) and I finally found out that he had went to his bank and claimed that I committed fraud by signing his name to the insurance check.

I have a clause in all my contracts that gives me a limited power of attorney which includes the signing of checks or any other documents on behalf of the homeowner. I did this to save a lot of time trying to run down the homeowner because many times, the insurance company will make the checks out to them and to me and mail the check to my office.

Little did I know, at the time, that he had used one of my old contracts that did not have the power of attorney and though it was an honest mistake, I not only had to give the homeowner back fourteen thousand dollars ($14,000.00), the judge hit me with a five thousand dollar ($5,000.00) penalty for signing his name to the check.

During this same time period, one of my Nashville estimators had a very large house fire that was being repaired and just absolutely did not do his job and the repairs drug out for almost two (2) years instead of the standard eight (8) months. I will say that the owner was very unusual in that though he had just cause to be upset, he never raised his voice to me. I finally fired him after giving him at least a dozen chances and talking to him until I was blue in the face. I took over this job and as it wound up, at the end of repairs, I felt that the owner owed me fifty five thousand dollars ($55,000.00) but he felt that he did not owe me any more than twenty thousand dollars ($20,000.00). I felt that he was a good honest man and I think that he felt the same about me and when we could not agree on the amount, I suggested that we revert to our contract and go to binding arbitration. As things stood at the time we went to arbitration, I showed a loss of over sixty thousand dollars ($60,000.00) on this job. Since this job was nearly a three hundred thousand dollar ($300,000) job, it is not only the sixty thousand dollars ($60,000.00) that I lost in actual money that included labor and material, it was also the lost profit that I would have made which would have been close to ninety thousand dollars ($90,000.00) because, I had a system set up where my estimators and branch managers receive ten percent (10%) of the gross amount collected on a job and I sub contracted the job for another sixty percent (60%) which left me with a guaranteed thirty percent (30%) profit on each job. So, the total amount that I actually lost was near one hundred fifty thousand dollars ($150,000.00). More about the arbitration case will be included later.

Again, during this same time period, my Shelbyville estimator was working with only one adjuster but, that adjuster was sending enough business that he made over one hundred thousand dollars ($100,000.00) a year plus he made me over one hundred thousand dollars ($100,000.00) a year. Murphy's Law was definitely in effect at this time because, the last thing that I expected to happen, happened. This adjuster went to another contractor and asked to borrow some money for an operation for his grandson and another adjuster in his office found out about it and told his supervisor, this caused him to be terminated. He was making me about ten thousand dollars ($10,000.00) a month which was about what my bills came to and so needless to say, that was quite a hit to my bank account.

In addition, the last and only job that he had left was some major repairs to a church from the tornado damage and I had the bad luck of having him quit during the work being done.

A few weeks prior to losing the adjuster, he had been torn with an idea of having these cabinets made that would fit interchangeably where you could have a bookcase or a console and you could move the cabinets around where they would all fit. This is difficult to explain unless you saw all the drawings however, he talked me into investing in the idea so, I gave him a total of eight thousand dollars ($8,000.00) over a several week period and about the time he lost the adjuster, I saw that it was going to take a lot more money than I had to get a factory set up and meet workers payroll and so, I stopped investing and when I did, he turned on me. He even refused to give me back my computer and fax machine.

He also did not watch over the church job that he had sub contracted. The sub contractor quit so, I did make a deal with one of my Nashville estimators since he was good with carpentry work to finish the job.

Without going into all the details, I wound up losing over forty thousand dollars ($40,000.00) on this job in actual money lost. Again, this is not taking into consideration the profits I would have made. This job was over two hundred thirty thousand dollars ($230,000.00) so, there went another sixty thousand dollars ($60,000.00) to seventy thousand dollars ($70,000.00).

Jane and I married in October 1996. My oldest daughter, Pamela married Eddie just a couple days apart from mine. Pamela (I call her Pammie) and Eddie bought a really nice home right on Kentucky lake at Paris, Tennessee. Eddie was in his mid twenties. They had dated for several years. Eddie had been living at home while working in a factory. Though he saved up quite a bit of money, he was unhappy so, Pammie asked me to teach Eddie my business.

I loaned him Jane's car and over a year period, I loaned them over thirty thousand dollars ($30,000.00). I believe the good ones will figure it out on their own with little help so, I verbally instructed him and I went on two house fires with him and that was it. I bought them a fax machine and a computer and gave him an insurance estimating system. Over the next few years, Eddie paid me back all that was owed and they had about anything they wanted. Pammie had four kids, Landon, Lake, Livia and Laina (Yeah, she must like the letter L. ha).

CHAPTER 5

DOING IT AGAIN

Before I finish this book and forget to tell you, no, I haven't filed bankruptcy twice. The title of the book is "From Bankruptcy To A Millionaire—Twice—A True Story". I've started out with nothing, bankrupt. I had a 1955 Chevrolet 2-door hardtop, a few clothes, and a job. That was it. I did file bankruptcy in 1982 after losing everything the first time. After losing everything the second time, I did not file bankruptcy, like most people would have and I did not do so because, I had learned that obtaining wealth is not something that just happens, it is something one learns and there is no doubt in my mind that I would become a millionaire again.

So, as I write this book, what has been going on?

Well, to pick up where I've left off in other chapters, after making my wife move out in February of 2002, I was left with very little money. I had enough to sustain me for about three or four months and did not have any income whatsoever. I got on the internet and applied for over one thousand two hundred (1,200) jobs as an insurance adjuster or estimator for contractors that do insurance repair work and though, I was much more qualified than most, I soon realized that no one wants to hire someone over the age of fifty.

No problem—or so I thought. I had that one job that had gone to arbitration in January of 2002 and I had received an award in that case and was fully expecting the other party to pay me the other sixty three thousand dollars ($63,000.00) that he owed. I had earlier found out that it is almost impossible to overturn an arbitration case so, I felt very good about the situation but, I got quite a surprise when I found out that this gentleman appealed the verdict. That appeal was heard in July of 2002 and I won again.

I thought that surely, he would go ahead and pay me now that he lost the appeal but, to my surprise again, he appealed to the state supreme court. I just recently, as of November 2005, got a verdict and I lost. Now, we have to start all over again because the umpire that made the ruling in this case did not give the other party the opportunity to have a hearing. So, in going back, I was totally dependent upon that money but, it did not come through.

About mid-summer of 2002, I decided to get back into the construction business and picked up several jobs but I did not have enough operating capital to carry these jobs until I could receive some money so, I had to borrow several thousand dollars from my oldest daughter.

To my surprise, this particular adjuster that I was working with got promoted and the adjuster that took over his position wanted to work with another contractor so, I lost that account. I made a few thousand dollars but, again, that money soon ran out. I then struggled for several months and in the fall of 2003, I was able to go work hurricane Isabel in Virginia and made enough money to sustain me for a few more months. However, in February of 2004, my luck ran out.

I was out of money and out of any income coming in. So, my truck was repossessed and so was my home. I was left walking with very little money.

I rented an efficiency apartment, not knowing how in the world I going to pay the next month's rent. If anyone had ever told me that I would seek financial help from the government, I would have told them that they were absolutely nuts and that things would never be that bad. However, I had to lower my pride and ask for food stamps. I used these for several months in order to eat. I did pick up scattered jobs where I would make two thousand dollars ($2000.00) to four thousand dollars ($4000.00) and that would carry me for a few more months. Then, in the fall of 2004 Hurricane Charlie hit Florida and I was able to do pretty well in adjusting claims in Orlando.

On the second day I was in Orlando, I went into a fast food restaurant and I saw a gentleman sitting at a booth with a cell phone and paperwork scattered on the table and just assumed he was an insurance adjuster. I found out that instead, he was a home improvement contractor.

After talking for a few minutes, he offered to carry me around Orlando for a couple of days until I got used to the layout of the city. Now, take into consideration that this contractor's phone was ringing off the wall yet, he took the time to help me out and that impressed me greatly.

The first day he rode me around, was on Thursday and late Friday afternoon, I said to him, "I do not want to embarrass you or put you on the spot but, I just have to know, are you a religious man?" He replied, "I am a Christian, why?" I said, "Because you didn't have to say anything, it just showed."

Several days later, he came by my motel room and asked me if I could help him and I told him that I would be glad to, what did he need?

He told me that he just assumed doing insurance repair work on things such as roofs, fences, drywall and such would be just like doing home improvement work but he did not understand all the insurance terminology about how "holdback" operated, how to submit a supplemental estimate on items the adjuster overlooked and other things and asked me if I knew how to do all that? I replied that I did.

He had several estimates that adjusters had written with him and I asked him to let me see one of them. In just a matter of a minute or so, I told him, after reviewing the estimate, that the adjuster has overlooked a lot of things on that estimate. He got wide-eyed and was surprised that I could pick up those items without ever going to the property. Anyway, after some discussion I told him that I would review all his estimates that he gets on his jobs, submit a supplemental estimate to the insurance company if, I found items that the adjuster overlooked and if I got them approved, I was to receive ten percent (10%) of the total amount that I found over and above what the insurance company had offered to the homeowner. He agreed.

As I later told him, when we had a disagreement, we are both old enough, we both know better than to make an agreement with anyone without putting it in writing. Yes, that was very stupid on my part to make a deal on a handshake because, it's so difficult months down the road to remember exactly what was said.

The agreement we made was that he was to give me a five hundred dollar ($500.00) a week draw three (3) weeks out of the month and a two thousand dollar ($2000.00) draw once a month.

He kept up his end of the agreement for many months but, in spite of my records showing that he still owed me around forty six thousand dollars ($46,000.00), his wife did not send my weekly draw check one week and, to keep a long story short, they did not feel that they owed me on any jobs where he did not collect his money.

I referred him back to what our agreement was, I get the supplement approved, I earn my money. His wife tried first, to say that I was a salesman on commission and after explaining to her that I did not sell anything, she backed off of that one. Now, here are two (2) people, he and his wife, that are supposed to be Christians. Take into consideration that, I shared documents and knowledge with him that I would not have done with anyone else and because of those forms of mine that he used and the knowledge that I shared with him, he made between one half and one and a half million dollars because he met me. I have found out that people will use any excuse in the world to try and justify greed.

To try and shorten this, he hired an attorney and I decided that I was going to get this matter settled without dragging it through the courts for years so, when I was on my way to Miami to work hurricane Wilma in the fall of 2005, I stopped by Orlando, called him and was able to make a settlement to just get the matter behind me. Here again, I decided to forgive him realizing that, a person will reap what they sow.

In the end, I was beat out of over twenty three thousand dollars ($23,000.00). Once I left Orlando the next morning, I refused to think about it any longer and just get on with my life as, I had done previously with the men who had beat me out of all that money in my construction business. People go around life dragging all those old dead dogs with them and by doing so, choose to be unhappy.

The money that I made from adjusting claims on hurricane Charlie along with the money I made with Dan allowed me to have a pretty decent lifestyle and allowed me to have the money to support myself when I went to work hurricane Wilma.

When I went to Miami to work hurricane Wilma, I had previously worked hurricane Andrew so, I knew that the streets in Miami were laid out much different than what I had been used to so to save myself time, I hired a taxi cab driver for one hundred dollars ($100.00) per day. I would set up ten (10) appointments and bring the files with me, get to the cab drivers home at six thirty AM and hand the files to him and he would line out the best route to go and I would be on someone's roof by 7 AM. In Miami, everything you have, had better be nailed down, bolted down, or locked because it would be gone when you came back if you didn't. When I stopped at someone's home, I would hand my truck keys to the cab driver and he would unlock my ladder, get it off the truck, and put it up against the house while I was taking a photo of the front of the house. After I came down off the roof, he would put the ladder back on my truck and come inside to help me hold one end of my measuring tape which also made things go faster and I used a tape recorder to also speed things up. By doing things this way, I was able to look at ten to twelve claims and be back to my motel by one to one thirty in the afternoon. During this time in Miami, I looked at one hundred forty seven (147) claims in six (6) weeks and closed all of them and came back home. Other adjusters were only looking at four (4) or five (5) claims a day and many of them that had fifty (50) to seventy-five (75) less claims than I did, were still there working in February of 2006. I cleared over sixty thousand ($60,000.00) which, a large part of that was used to repay debts and money that I owed.

In February of 2006, I saw that if I did not do something that my money would run out before the next hurricane season so, I came up with the idea of making contact with people in New Orleans Louisiana and offering to review their estimates that they had received from their adjusters from hurricane Katrina and do so free of charge then, if I found items that the adjuster overlooked and felt like I could get them more money, I designed a contract I could send to them. I got my mailing list from the white pages on the internet.

As I am writing this book off and on, I am still working on these and it is now February of 2007. Presently, I have nine (9) clients that I will make anywhere between two thousand

($2,000.00) and ten thousand ($10,000.00) on each one. The insurance commissioner in Louisiana has given people a year extension so, I know I can do this until August 29, 2007 however, I am using part of that money to fund other ideas and projects I am working on which, of course, writing books is part of that. I have one book titled, "Why No Money Down Real Estate Really Does Work", a hardback version that, will came out in two weeks. Once I finish this present book that you are reading, I will also submit it to the publisher. Yes, I realize hitting a number one best-seller or a good-selling book is extremely difficult. I have found that it is one thing to write a good book but it's another thing to promote the book where the general public is aware of it where it will sell good. I have an idea for a couple of web sites. One is where I will give people an alternative when they have a civil matter against someone else and can go to binding arbitration instead of going to a high-priced attorney, in my opinion, that will run a big bill up on them and will sometimes take months or years to get through the court systems. My set-up will allow people to get their civil matter settled within thirty (30) days time at a fraction of the cost of an attorney, in my opinion, yet; the decision by the umpire will be just as binding and just as legal as if any judge or jury made the award.

I have another website where I am designing courses that will teach people how to obtain wealth.

In calculating my first idea, I based my figures on some of the popular TV judges that handle two (2) cases per hour and they do this, in spite of many coming into the courtroom and running the other one down about their drug use and their sex life and everything else and in my set-up, that will not be allowed. So, I know that two (2) cases per hour could be heard and based on my fee schedule just for my state, assuming I have an office in every county, I will clear fifty eight million dollars ($58,000,000.00) a year just in one state. Hey, maybe it won't work but, this is not some pie-in-the-sky dream or some scheme and what if it only works half as good as I think it will? You're darn right, it's worth a try. I am thoroughly convinced that if you have a product, a service or knowledge to sell, all you have to is build a good website with good links, go to the mailbox and go to the bank. Yes, I could get back into the insurance claims repair business and I admit, sometimes, it is very tempting since, everyone is always saying that I am the best there is at that business but, hey, I don't need all that drama and stress in my life and will avoid doing so as long as I can. Besides, I want to be able to say that I became a millionaire in more than one field. I think you see, I have a lot of good ideas but, it takes time for your efforts to pay off. I have made over one hundred thousand dollars ($100,000.00) the past year but, that isn't near what I use to make. I know that most people would be more than happy with the present income I have but, I am so driven that, it is not good enough for me. I will not ever be satisfied unless I'm always going for the gold and giving it my best shot. I don't doubt at all, that I will have other book ideas and other ways of making money. I don't doubt at all, that I could make a very good living in the real estate business however, though I love helping people and I care about other people I've also learned that they become very greedy, whether they're Christians or not when money is thrown into the equation. So, I prefer not to deal with people.

For those of you that got wide-eyed when I was talking about making ten thousand dollars ($10,000.00) per week as an independent storm adjuster and you want to know how to do that then, I will tell you how to do that. All you have to do to get started is to get on the internet and look up some of the major insurance companies as; they will send you to school to teach you how to be an adjuster. After two (2) or three (3) years experience working with them and you are the driven type then you can go on your own and work nothing but storms. If you are the type that does not want responsibility on your own and prefer to work for someone else then, you will make much more than the national average plus, you will be furnished with a car to drive. Learning about adjusting claims will also give you knowledge enough to start your own construction company later on if you so choose.

In the fall of 2007, hurricane Ike hit the Texas coast and as far inland as Houston, there was considerable wind damage. Nothing really big, just mostly shingles blown off, fences down & carports damaged. I first went to Dallas for an orientation with an independent adjusting firm. I was shocked because I knew more than the man giving the instructions. I also found out that there were nearly two hundred (200) people in the room who had never adjusted a claim before. That frightened me because I knew those adjusters were going to get a lot of complaints so, I wondered if the insurance companies would pay the adjusting firm where I would get paid. I decided that I didn't want to work for a company that was putting people out there and didn't know what they were doing so, the next morning, on my way to Houston from Dallas, I decided to get a motel in Houston and call other adjusting firms.

I ran across a public adjuster that was interested in my services. A public adjuster is an adjuster that represents the homeowner against their insurance company and usually charges ten (10) to fifteen (15) percent of their total claim. The first assignment he gave me was water damage to a seventeen (17) story apartment complex that had damage to about ninety percent (90%) of all of the apartments. It took me three weeks to go in each apartment, measure each room and tape record the damages and in the evenings and weekends, I would enter the information in my computer. The estimate was over four hundred pages. The insurance company hired an independent adjusting firm to do their estimate. They sent out two (2) experienced adjusters who, both had an engineer's degree. The other adjusters estimate was, nine hundred thousand dollars ($900,000.00). The final settlement was, one million, nine hundred thousand dollars ($1,900,000.00) so, I got the owner over one million dollars ($1,000,000.00) more than he was first offered. Yeah, I am pretty darned good at that type work.

I made a lot of money on that one claim plus, the public adjuster gave me several other claims to work so, I stayed in Houston several months.

CHAPTER 6

BRAIN WASHED

I suppose brain washed is a term I personally use for one's prejudice views on different subjects.

A few years ago, I did some basic financial planning for middle class people and conducted some public seminars and one of my main points, at the beginning, was that nearly eighty seven percent (87%) of all Americans at the age of sixty five (65) and older retire in poverty. Why?

It really boils down to the fact that we are all brain washed to one degree or another. Oh, so you don't think you are huh? Well, let me give you a quick test and we will see.

I bet I am right ninety percent (90%) of the time when I say if, in religion, your mom and/or dad was Catholic, Baptist, Methodist or so on, I bet I can tell you what your religion is. After you graduated from high school/college and started making your own money if, your mom or dad had their car/truck insurance with ABC insurance company, I bet I can tell you who you have insurance with. How am I doing so far?

I bet again that, when you graduated and got your first job and opened your first bank account if, mom and dad banked at XYZ bank, I will bet I can tell you where you bank at.

Still think you are not brain washed? You see, our subconscious mind is sort of like programming a computer. What goes in comes out. Negative thoughts and negative thinking will produce negative words that come out of your mouth. Positive thoughts and thinking will produce positive words that come out of your mouth. We have the attitude in America that if it is good enough for mom and dad, it is good enough for me and that is just the way people think. We usually do not stop to challenge what we have been taught to believe and usually if someone else challenges us, we will defend what we have been brought up to believe with every fiber in us.

I have often said that, you could walk into a bar, meet two (2) drunks that have not been inside a church building in twenty (20) years, start discussing religion with them and if, one was brought up to believe that water Baptism was necessary to be saved and the other person did not believe that it was necessary and they got into a discussion on the subject, the fur would fly in a matter of minutes and they would nearly wind up in a fist fight.

Likewise, people who retire in poverty do so because, they follow their parents' footsteps of saving with a bank or life insurance policy and that just will not get it. Why? Because, for instance, if you're getting five percent (5%) interest on your savings and that particular year's rate of inflation is also five percent (5%) then, you in essence, are not making one penny because inflation is eating up the interest that is earned.

I hope by inserting this section, it will help you realize how close minded most of us are to accepting something different because, when someone comes along and says something different as I mentioned above, it most certainly will be opened to criticism and especially if someone says something that most of us consider radical.

Basically, no one likes to be told that they are wrong and there are very few of us because of our stupid pride, will admit that we are wrong. This, in most cases, is even with overwhelming evidence staring us in the face.

There are very few people who are open minded enough to challenge something they have been taught or believed all of their lives and this especially applies to one's religious and financial view point. It is extremely difficult to get someone to change.

My main purpose with this chapter, is to open your mind to the fact that, all of us are literally brain washed about not only religion, finance, insurance, careers and many other areas of life and we don't even realize it.

A few years ago, I did some basic financial planning for middle class people. I taught people some basic financial principles that a sixth (6th) grader would have to have help to misunderstand and was about as common sense as you could get. The information that I gave them was backed up by dozens of articles and books by true consumerist that said the same exact thing yet, most people wouldn't change what they were doing in spite of all of that evidence right in front of them. Why? Because, for decades, things have been done the way they have been doing things financially and this is the way they were taught though, it was the wrong way.

Needless to say, as far as making a living doing financial planning, I about starved to death in that line of work and swore to myself-Never Again!

I recall doing one of those financial planning seminars in a hotel once and at the beginning of the seminar, I stated that if, time permitted, at the end, I would show them how to purchase real estate with no money down. To my surprise, this middle aged man jumped up from his seat and shouted, "Mister, I don't know what kind of scam you have got going here but, I have been selling real estate for twenty five (25) years and I have never had anyone willing to sell their property for no money down."

This of course, caught me completely off guard and I figured immediately if, I didn't reply in a firm and positive way, I would lose the attention of my audience. Actually, everyone getting up and walking out quickly flashed through my mind.

Trying to be nice but firm, I said, "Sir that is because you didn't ask." You see, this gentleman, as with most people, had assumed anyone would be crazy to sell their property for no money down but, when you read my book, "Why no Money Down Real Estate Really Does Work,", you will soon realize that there are a lot of "crazy" people out there. I know first hand because; I have purchased several pieces of property over the years with little or no money down.

In the sales business of every kind, you have to open your mouth and ask for information along with asking for the sale. I promise you, that ninety nine percent (99%) of all realtors that you would call at random would think you were absolutely nuts if, you asked them about purchasing property for no money down. Talk about being brain washed! You see, not meaning to put anyone down, anyone with three hundred dollars ($300.00) and an eighth ($8^{th}$) grade level of intelligent can pass the real estate exam. Then, you can take another three hundred dollars ($300.00) for clothes in order to look the part and then, you can sit in an office of a well known realtor by the telephone and list clients and sell them or, you can list family and friends in order to sell their properties but does that make you a realtor?

Once they have a listing then, they hope to find a buyer that has a big enough down payment plus one that can also qualify. How sad.

These new agents quickly get brain washed into the same old traditional way of selling real estate and are absolutely closed minded to any other way. What other way?

Someone once wrote that, you can get anything you want in life, if you help enough other people get what they want—first. Let's apply that saying here.

What does the seller want? She/he wants a fair market value for their home and they want their equity out of their home. The real estate agent wants their commission and so does the broker. The key to all of the above getting what they want, lies with the buyer and so, if, the seller has ten thousand dollars ($10,000.00) equity in the home, wants it out and the buyer doesn't have that kind of money sorry, no deal. The real estate agent keeps looking.

Give me a break! Who has ten thousand dollars ($10,000.00) sitting around in a savings account and is twenty-one (21) to forty-one (41) years old? No one I ever met.

The buyers' problem is almost always the down payment so, for the seller to resolve his/her problem and for the real estate agent to resolve his/her problem they must do some creative thinking and come up with some creative financing to meet their goals.

No, this will not work all the time but, it will work most of the time if, people will just open their minds (offers) to give both parties what they want but, maybe not exactly when they want it. Everyone can get what they want but, they must be flexible in their wants.

I won't keep you in suspense any longer. Here is a typical no-money-down deal.

As the buyer, you are looking for a motivated seller i.e., a person who is anxious to get rid of their property. This usually means the seller has been transferred to another city or state because of their work, someone who is going through a divorce, and someone who is laid off from work or who has various other financial problems. No, I am not talking about taking advantage of people I am talking about people who will be more flexible and who are open to creative ideas.

I would hunt people who fit the categories above from newspaper ads, dealing directly with them, thereby, eliminating the commissions of a realtor.

Let's say, I found a seller who, had been transferred to another state and I assumed that he/she had an average income plus, his/her mate also works. I can assume this by the price and the location of the house for sale.

Now, I can pretty well know that he/she has a payment at their new location that, they have been transferred to a new location or are paying a sizeable amount in rent plus, the additional amount they have on their house for sale. Bingo! They are in a financial bind or soon will be because; they cannot afford both payments for very long. I need to help him/her solve their problem!

Let's say his/her house has a value of one hundred thousand dollars ($100,000.00) and his/her equity is fifteen thousand dollars ($15,000.00) and he/she does not have to have the equity out of the house right now. Remember, if, he/she sold me their house they would pay about five thousand dollars ($5,000.00) in closing costs, leaving them ten thousand dollars ($10,000.00).

My offer to them is full market value for the house on a lease/ purchase option for seven (7) years. I always want to use one of my own contracts. I always use one of my own contracts because; it has an escape clause so that if things don't go the way I expect, I can get out of the deal. I can make the deal subject to my attorney's approval, my partner's approval, etc, etc. This will give me an escape if, things do not go the way I expected.

Why seven (7) years? Because, on the average, homes double in value every seven (7) years. I definitely do not want a deal where I will get less than a five (5) year lease.

Another reason I want to use my own contract is because, I want a clause in the contract that allows me to sub-let the house to someone else because, that is exactly what I plan on doing.

This may surprise you but, I will be willing to pay the home owners insurance coverage, land taxes and take care of all the maintenance. Why? Here's why. One, I am on a lease with a purchase option, I am in the driver's seat at the end of the lease. If, the lease does not go as I planned, I have the option to not close for the purchase price but, if, things do go as planned; the seller has to sell it. Two (2), let's say at the end of the seven (7) years things do not go well as I had hoped. Instead of the house being worth two hundred thousand dollars ($200,000.00); let's say that the house is only worth one hundred and fifty thousand dollars ($150,000.00); I just made fifty thousand dollars ($50,000.00).

Now, wait a minute, what about the eight hundred dollar ($800.00) payment that needs to be made each month?

On a home of this size, I should be able to get twelve hundred dollars ($1,200.00) a month on a lease with a purchase option and with the extra four hundred dollars ($400.00) each month; I can pay the home owners insurance, land taxes, and maintenance expenses. The maintenance is primarily for electrical, heating, and air conditioning and you can bet that, I checked those out before I made the deal so that, I won't have any expenses on these items.

So, let's see where I am at after seven years. I have a house worth one hundred and fifty thousand dollars ($150,000.00), someone else lived in that house and made my payments for me and I decided that, I want to buy that house at closing so; we first do a double-close. I close on my contract with the seller then; I close on my contract with my buyer. Please check with a real estate attorney before you attempt to do a double-close because, in some states, this is illegal. I have made fifty thousand dollars ($50,000.00). The seller got what he/she wanted, my buyer got what they wanted, and I made a bundle without messing anyone over. This of course, assumes that, I sold the house to my renter because; I also put them on a lease with a purchase option contract. So I sold the house for one hundred and fifty thousand dollars ($150,000.00) to my buyer and I gave one hundred thousand dollars ($100,000.00) for the property. Now, for the negative thinking type person, what if, I was fifty percent (50%) off on my estimation and only made twenty-five thousand dollars ($25,000.00) but, let's say I made one of those deals a month. That is three hundred thousand dollars ($300,000.00) a year income so, what if, I had to call one hundred people to find one deal like this? Do you think that you would like to make one deal like this a month? Oh, by the way, you can do this without any money or any credit.

I promise you that deals like this are done all the time. Now, do you still think that real estate cannot be purchased without any money down? If, this causes your light bulb to come on then, you certainly need to order my book "Why No Money Down Real Estate Really Does Work"-Amazon.com, Barnes & Noble.com or, iUniverse.com.

Remember the title of this particular chapter? If, you doubt what I stated previously about mentioning no money down to a realtor then, I challenge you to call up any realtor in the country and ask them if, they have any property which you can purchase like this or any no-money-down deals and I promise you they will think that you're crazy. In most leases with a purchase option homes available to a realtor, the realtor will push for you putting a sizable amount of money down on the lease. This is very standard among realtors.

No, this book is not about real estate, I wrote it, in hopes to open up your mind to opportunities right in front of you and all you need to do is educate yourself a little bit outside the normal realm of going to college or going to some trade school. Read everything that you can find at the library in regards to people that have become wealthy and learn how they did it because, obtaining wealth is something you learn, not something that just happens.

Getting people to redirect their mind and be open-minded to receive new information is extremely difficult and even tradition plays a major role in developing one's thinking.

A classic example of this tradition is the typical way which funerals are held and the senseless heartache associated with it. Many years ago, when my father died, knowing that my mother knew half the people in the county which she resided, I knew as each person came into the funeral home, my mom would have to go up to the casket and go through a painful and emotional experience, each time. Wanting to spare my mom of this pain, I suggested something very unusual. I asked her about closing the casket for visiting and for the actual services and told her why. First, I told mom about dad never liking anyone who stared at him and that dad's memory was in my mind not in a coffin but, if she and my two sisters wanted to view the body one last time before the services began that was up to them. Personally, I do not want to view any dead body, I don't care whose it is.

Mom accepted my suggestion and I can't tell you how much easier the services were on her and also, us children. To this day and as long as I live, I will not walk up to the coffin of someone I cared about and put myself through that needless emotional pain which, immediately follows. The dead are dead and the living must move on. Personally, I have made plans ahead of time and have already given instructions that, when I die, my body is to be taken and buried immediately. I have instructed that, my family is to have a celebration.

I have instructed in my will that, I do not want those old sad songs played; don't want any preacher putting me in Heaven or hell. I want them to serve peel and eat shrimp, wine, cheese, and finger food. I want them to stop for two to three minutes while one song is played in my memory. That song is Elvis Presley's version of, "I Did It My Way".

Since my father's death, approximately twenty-five (25) years ago at this writing, I have not been back to a cemetery and I do not plan on going to one until my mother is buried and I will not go to one again.

Heartless? No, just the opposite. Getting over the passing of someone you love is not that much different than getting over a divorce. If, you keep seeing the person you are divorcing or that is divorcing you, you will never get over that person. If, you keep pictures and things that remind you of that person all over your house, it will be very difficult to get on with your life. My father is deceased and I will have to accept that and get on with my life and stop punishing myself and putting myself through emotional unpleasantness by continued graveyard visiting.

The typical funeral is conducted the way it is, because the general public accepts it. It is a brainwashing of acceptance. Don't you realize that some funeral homes take advantage of people when their emotions are high?

Needless to say, you figured out by now by what you have read so far that, I do a lot of things in my life that are not traditional. I have never been ordinary or average, I hope never to be so. I am one of these people that have to go for the gold all the time. Anything else and I would not be happy with myself.

It is sort of like writing this book. I'm sure you have noticed in this one, or if you have read any of my other one's, that they are done a little different from the traditional way. Why? Well, where is the instruction manual of what to say in a book such as this? Who says that I'm not supposed to put certain things in a book? Heck, I am the author and will write whatever I want, especially since; I am initially paying to have it published.

My whole purpose of including this chapter is so that, you can see somewhat, how the subconscious mind works. I also want you to have at least some idea that, more than likely, you are prejudice in your religious views and traditions and hopefully, by including this chapter you will have a more open mind in regards to the things that, you will face in the game of life.

One of the major brain-washing of acceptance subjects that I want to bring your attention to is education. In America, we are brain-washed into thinking that, get out of high school, go to college, equals success. Wrong. I am a common-sense type person and since the fact that over eighty seven percent (87%) of all Americans age sixty-five (65) and over, retires in poverty, that tells me that going to college, for the most part, doesn't work, retirement programs don't work, savings with a bank or insurance company don't work, etc, etc, etc. What does work? Before I get to the answer on that, I want to stick with what I just said for a moment. If, what I just said surprises you, then, let me ask you a few questions. Since you've been out of high school, how many frogs have you dissected? How many sentences have you diagrammed? How many Algebra or Geometry problems have you worked? Are you beginning to see what I mean? In addition, most people that do have a college degree are not working in the field that they went to school and spent four years out of their life and all that money to learn. I have learned, over the years, that in attending college classes, nearly half of the classes that they are required to take has absolutely nothing to do with the field that they're studying to be. The way that our education system is, people that do not have the money or do not have the knowledge to attend college, are left flipping hamburgers at one of the fast food joints. We need to do like some of the other countries and have two years of high school and then a person selects a trade if, they know they are not going to college. By trades, I mean electrician, plumber, air conditioning, etc. We need to train people on how to make a living. You see, college will give you knowledge but, it does not teach you about the real world. What I am trying to get across to you is, when you have a free enterprise system, like we do in America, and you're willing to pay the price and by paying the price, I mean you're willing to bust your rear and do things that the other people are not willing to do like, working sixteen to seventeen hours a day (seven days a week), giving up watching their favorite TV programs, etc. in order to succeed. If those two fit your life, then, there is only one thing left to get you on your way to becoming wealthy and that is, finding the right vehicle to take you there. By vehicle I mean it may be the real estate business, construction, finance, or many other areas that you can become self-employed in. There is one other thing and that is time. It takes time for your efforts to pay off. I went over what I did in order to prepare your mind for what I am about to say.

As you have seen, the subconscious mind is indeed, a very fascinating thing.

Years ago, I read a book in regards to the subconscious mind and being a common-sense type person, the author made a couple of statements that just really stuck in my mind. He said that, if, a man or a woman can use their hands to break block, brick or boards without injuring their hand and can walk on hot coals without even getting a burn on their feet, what else can the subconscious do?

Shortly after reading that book, one Sunday afternoon, my ex-wife and myself were supposed to go to some friends' home for dinner along with several other couples but, the flu hit me like a ton of bricks and I asked her to just go along by herself. Not feeling very well, I laid down in the bed and started thinking about that book and so, I decided to give it a try. I concentrated on using my mind to heal my body. Usually, when somebody has the flu, it takes someone several days to get over it where, they can get out of bed and function at all. Once someone is to that stage, it still takes three (3) or four (4) days to get back to one hundred percent (100%).

I got up the next morning and as I said to my ex-wife, I felt like going bear hunting with a switch. I had never felt so good in my life. That was over thirty-five (35) years ago and I have not been in the bed sick with the flu nor had to go to the doctor in all these years. Yes, when I do feel the flu coming on I drink a lot of liquids and take heavy doses of vitamin c but mainly, I use my mind to heal myself.

Back during that particular time, when I told people about doing that and that I believed a person can learn to use their mind to heal themselves of anything, of course, I was laughed at.

Well, people aren't laughing anymore because doctors are now using that very same technique to teach people how to heal themselves and many people that were diagnosed as having terminal cancer have been completely healed and the cancer is completely gone. One of the major news channels had a story in this regard. One lady in particular was given six months or less to live and the doctor told her about this technique so, not having anything at all to lose, she decided to try it. The doctor showed her the old Atari video Pac Man game and told her to picture the white corpuscle cells as the good guys that were eating up the bad corpuscle cells. She did this once per day, not really believing anything would happen. When she went back up for her monthly check-up, the cancer was in remission and the doctor, even though he told her about this, was also astonished. She thought well, if once a day did all that good she would do it four or five times a day. When she went back for her next month's check-up, the cancer was completely gone. This was an actual case and reflects many others that since have been cured by using their mind.

There is a story in the book of Matthew in the bible, which tells about Jesus healing the blind man. Now, here is the son of God that could have completely healed this man by just speaking words but he did not do that. He touched the man's eyes and when the man opened them, Jesus asked him what he could see. The blind man replied that he could see images of trees and men. Now a little common sense if this man had been blind from birth, he would not know what trees and men looked like. It's odd what the next thing that Jesus did. He spit in the blind man's eyes. Now, why would he do that? You wouldn't know unless you knew, during that time, the Jews believed there was miraculous healing power in saliva. Yes, you have it figured out. This man was not blind from birth but had blinded his own self by his own mind.

The whole point I'm trying to get across to you is the mind is the only thing in this life that you can control. You can decide the thoughts that go into your mind and your mind works just like a computer, whatever goes in is going to come out. So, to those of you who fill your minds with negative things, hang around with people who have negative attitudes about life and tell you that you can't become wealthy or you can't do this or that, it boils down to garbage is in your mind so garbage will come out of your mouth.

There are millions of people that go to a doctor because of some tragedy in their life i.e., going through a divorce, a death in the family, loss of a job, etc. A doctor, will give them a pill to take when they get up in the morning, one for during the day, and one before they go to bed at night because he makes money off of giving you those drugs so you become addicted to drugs instead of facing life's problems and dealing with them. Almost every day is going to bring problems. Is it pleasant to deal with them? Of course not. Don't cop out of the game of life by popping a pill or seeking the bottle for a drink. You can learn how to deal with problems by refusing to think about unpleasant things that have happened to you. Sure, everyone gets depressed momentarily. Just don't stay there. Catch yourself thinking negative thoughts or worrying about things that you can do absolutely nothing about and decide that you are going to refuse to think about those negative things.

Along the lines of this subject of brainwashing, I want to give you one of the most eye-opening things your have ever heard in your entire life. According to the U.S. Census Bureau, nearly eighty-seven percent of Americans age sixty-five or older retire in poverty. We are in the richest country in the world, so what is the problem with our seniors retiring in such dire straits?

It is because we have not been taught properly, how money works and we have been fed nothing but bologna sandwiches in regard to education. Let me show you what I am talking about. As I just mentioned, nearly eighty-seven (87%) percent of all retirees retire in poverty. Now, I don't know what that tells you but it tells me real quick, savings with a bank or insurance company does not work, retirement programs at work do not work and, for the most part, going to college does not work. What? Let me show you what I am talking about. When my daughters were teenagers, I once said this at my mother's house in front of her to my daughters, "as far as I am concerned, other than reading, writing, and arithmetic, going to high school and grammar school was a total waste of my time." My mother had a fit that I said something like that in front of them so, I asked her since she had been out of high school how many frogs she had dissected, how many sentences she had diagrammed and how many algebra problems she had worked? Kids are going to college and almost half or more of the subjects they are required to take have absolutely nothing to do with their chosen career.

When considering college, not only is it the cost of going that has to be considered, it's also what that person could've made if they were still working. So assuming college costs approximately fifty thousand ($50,000) in the year 2007 that I am recording this, a person could make at least fifteen ($15,000) a year times four years so that's another sixty thousand ($60,000). So, at the best, when a person graduates from college they're at least one hundred and ten ($110,000) in the hole. Now let's say, a person gets a job that they earn ten thousand ($10,000) more than the average person makes because of their degree, it will take them eleven years to just get even. So if the average college graduate is twenty-three (23) years old they will be thirty-four (34) years old when they get even, then they will live like anyone else. Week to week, paycheck to paycheck. They will be an average of five thousand dollars ($5,000) in debt with credit cards and all of their remaining income will go to food, clothing, and shelter and the only basic difference is that they may have a little bit nicer car and a little bit bigger house. Not only all of this, they just used four years of their life and years where they were young and in their prime.

Now, let's back up and catch those that don't go to college. Most of those are doing the jobs that no one else will do such as flipping hamburgers, cleaning, and trash hauling and such. Now, don't get me wrong, I think education is great as long as you're taught about the real world such as real estate, finance, construction and such things.

Years ago, I learned that one country has two (2) years of what we would call high school then the student selects a trade they think they would like such as electrician, accountant, plumber, and other service-oriented field. They go for one (1) year and if they still want to pursue that particular path, then they continue a second year. If not, they can switch careers and choose some other field.

I had an uncle that is now deceased, that put shoes on Tennessee walking horses and had shod five world champions and he was so good that men were willing to come in from all across the country to learn from him and were willing to work for him for nothing for a year or more in order to learn the trade. Now, what if the local school systems got with contractors and other trades and furnished them a student for a year that they do not have to pay just so the student can learn the trade? Would this not make a difference in tens of thousands of lives?

In the game of life, you are going to work hard somewhere all of your life. When I asked myself a question at the age of twenty-three (23), was I getting paid what I thought I was worth, I clearly answered no. As I said earlier, I am a common-sense person, not a book person. All I had to do was look around me at my mother and father, relatives and friends. They all were, just like you are and just like you see others around you. They are all fighting, what I call the rat race with no way to win. Oh sure, if you're going to be a doctor, an attorney, or something like that where you can get out of college and within a matter of a short time start making over one hundred thousand ($100,000.00) a year then college should be they way you should go. But, unless you just have some personal hang-up and like something so much that you just want to pursue that particular career, even though it doesn't pay much, knock yourself out.

Also in the game of life, you have two choices as far as your chosen career. One, you can work for someone else. If you do that and you live in any-sized city at all, every day of your life you will have to get up early in the morning, rush to get ready, fight rush hour traffic, spend ten (10) or twelve (12) hours or more of your time sitting in traffic jams and at traffic lights per week and repeat that for forty (40) plus years. Every day that you come to work it's because someone told you to come to work, someone tells you when to take a break, someone tells you when you can go to lunch, someone tells you when you can get off, someone tells you when you can take a vacation and someone even tells you when you can retire. With the U.S. Census Bureau's figures as I have earlier quoted, more than likely you are going to be in that eighty-seven percent (87%). Now, there is a much better way if you choose to work for someone else. You had better learn how money works and I am specifically talking about compound interest, most people have no idea. It is probably the most important thing that you will ever learn in your whole life. Here's what I'm talking about. Most people think for instance, if they're getting six percent rate of return on their money and they go somewhere else and put their money where they can get twelve percent (12%) they would be doing twice as good because two (2) times six (6) is twelve (12). Wrong. Compound interest does not work that way. I assure you banks and insurance companies know exactly how it works. Just look downtown at any city, who owns the biggest buildings that you see? Now the critical part is understanding that unless you put your money somewhere where the interest rate is higher than the rate of inflation then, you are not making anything. For instance, let's say that you're getting four percent (4%) rate of return on your savings account and this year's inflation is four percent (4%) then, you are not making a penny. This is because the rate of inflation is eating up your buying power. Most people do not understand how compound interest works so, they do not understand that a small amount of money (and I'm talking about money that they would spend going out for one meal for a couple) and doing it per month would make them wealthy at retirement. For instance, setting aside just fifty dollars ($50.00) a month in a good-performing mutual fund would yield them approximately one million dollars ($1,000,000.00) at retirement. So there is no reason for anyone in America to wind up broke at retirement if they were taught some of these simple, basic principles. Yes, there are many more avenues than a mutual fund. Personally, I wish I had known about them and how they operated when I was in my early twenties and if I had, today I would not be worried about a thing. I make good so I don't worry anyhow but, if I worked a normal job I would be very concerned.

I am going to explain to you, in brief, a little bit about a mutual fund and why I like them so much. Let's say that you had a half million dollars available to invest. So, you could pick some of the top-named companies in the U.S., maybe automobile stock, insurance, manufacturing and others. You play the stock market. So by spreading your money around you get your flexibility and you realize that some stocks do well one year but, not in another. They will fluctuate so do not panic when something goes bad because it will go back up and what you're doing is making a commitment to leave your money there no matter what happens and you're looking for at least a five (5) to ten (10) year period. Preferably much longer. Now, let's say instead of spreading your money around you decide to put it all in one basket so to speak because that company had always done good. But the last thing you had expected, for the owner or president of the company to die, his kids take over, and ruin the company. You just lost all of your money. A mutual fund is insured by the federal government for five hundred thousand ($500,000.00) against fraud on the part of the mutual fund company. When you purchase a mutual fund, it allows a small investor with fifty (50) to a hundred dollars ($100.00) a month to get the same high rates of return that large investors get. The money is pooled together with thousands of other investors and the mutual fund manager takes that money and goes out on the stock market and purchases the stock. At this writing, mutual funds have been around for about seventy (70) years and the amazing part is not the first mutual fund company has ever gone under. Now, if you're looking for a worst-case scenario, ninety percent (90%) of this country's banks went under in the last depression. Mutual fund companies were around during the depression so if you are looking for safety, I don't think you could be any safer. Yes, there is a risk that you take but there is a lot of difference between a calculated risk and going out to Las Vegas and sticking your money in a slot machine.

A mutual fund is certainly not the only way a person, over time, can accumulate wealth. Each person has to decide what they do and do not like. However, the problem is when you start into college and at that young age, you don't know what's available so unless you were around real estate, construction, finance, investments, and things like that you have no idea which way to go.

Since the good Lord is not making anymore real estate and the population keeps getting bigger and bigger, even though it fluctuates according to the economy, real estate presents one of the best opportunities for people in America especially, those who do not attend college or could not afford to go, to become wealthy.

In order to change your life, and the wrong direction that you're going, you must first change your thinking that's the reason why I put this chapter in this book. If I was starting all over again, my common sense would tell me that if I wanted to become wealthy I would need to learn from other people since this is not taught in any college or school. I would suggest strongly that you read the following books which you can find in your local library and read them in the order that I have them listed. The first book is the book that absolutely changed my life because it changed my thinking and it got me thinking that when you're in a free-enterprise system, like we have in America, the only thing keeping one from being wealthy is them. That book is, "See You at the Top" by Zig Ziglar. The second book I would recommend is "Think and Grow Rich" by Napoleon Hill. Mr. Hill studied the lives of millionaires over a twenty-year period and he wrote down in this book the common denominators that caused these people to become wealthy. The third book is a tremendous book about finance, insurance, and real estate because the author wrote the book in easy to understand language and the name of that book is "The Power of Money Dynamics" by Venita Van Caspel. If I recall correctly, Ms. Van Caspel was voted the nation's number one financial planner out of Houston Texas somewhere around 1984 or 1985 and had her own show on public television. She is a tremendously brilliant woman and has several other books in the money dynamic series but this particular one is my favorite.

I will deal with the other choice you have in the game of life which is being self-employed in the next chapter.

CHAPTER 7

OPPORTUNITIES YOU CAN'T SEE, YET

During my time in Miami, working hurricane Andrew, I handled a claim on a Cuban American and one day, he stated to me "Ron, I love America more than you do". I said to him, "Well, that would have to be a lot because, I am extremely patriotic, having been a former sergeant in the army". He explained that when he was nineteen (19) years old that, he fought on the side of Castro, in Cuba until, he found out that Castro was a communist and that he and others had been deceived. He said that they built a raft and wound up in New York and he said that, he took jobs that no one else wanted and he worked two jobs, using one to pay bills and the other one to save every penny so that, he could go into business for his self and was doing bus boy jobs, mopping, sweeping and taking out trash and things like that and he explained if he, not knowing how to speak our language for five years, could become a millionaire what was my problem? Very good point I told him. I also told him that I had become a millionaire at one time. In case you don't know, it doesn't make any difference how much you owe if, you have a million dollars worth of assets which can be a combination of personal property, accountants' receivables and your property that you own, you are still considered a millionaire.

About twenty five (25) years ago, I kept an article out of a Nashville newspaper where a woman whose husband had left her for a younger woman and was left without any child support for her two children and was living in what I refer to, as a cracker box house or, in other words, one of those small houses that was built in the 1940's that generally has asbestos siding and has a detached garage that you can barely get a small vehicle in. One day, she got an idea about going into business for herself and though, she did not have very much money and was barely making ends meet, she hired an electrician to put in two or three florescent lights and she went to the lumber company and got a hammer, nails, plywood, 2 x 4's and some soding soil and the news paper stated that this lady was making seventy five thousand dollars ($75,000.00) a year and you will never believe what she was doing. She was growing alfalfa sprouts for health food stores out of that garage.

While dating Janie, she was working as a cosmetic sales lady in a major department store and was amazed at my business knowledge and was always wanting to learn and though her income was twice what any other women made, she was very unhappy working for someone else and she asked me why was I always talking about opportunity being right in front of people and they couldn't see it. I replied that, I was going to give her an idea or two so I asked her, being a single man, what did men like me living in an apartment (at that time) hate the most? Bingo! Cleaning, washing clothes and grocery shopping. So, I told her to put on her high heels, stockings and full make-up and take someone with her for security purposes and go in the afternoon after men got home from work, knock on their door and offer to clean their apartment for so much money. Then once you have some apartments, hire another woman to help her and once she is trained properly how to clean, it is time to knock on some more doors and get her some more business. Now, hire someone else to put with the woman that she trained and hire someone new to train herself and keep on repeating that process. I asked her how many apartments did she think are in the US and Canada, Great Britain and other free world countries? So in other words, she could become a millionaire by cleaning apartments if, she could get enough of other people working for her starting with thirty dollars ($30.00) of supplies. Just a matter of time.

Several years ago, my company was doing a repair on a home in a small town outside of Nashville and this town is known world wide because of the nursery business where, they ship trees and shrubs all over the world. In talking with the lady that owned the house one day, she told me about a neighbor of hers that was eighty four (84) years old and was making over two hundred and fifty thousand dollars ($250,000.00) a year out of her backyard because, I had asked why this women had all these shrubs, flowers and trees in her backyard with all those sand boxes that she had.

One day, I saw one of those real estate gurus advertising on television to give me a free seminar at a major hotel on Tuesday night and he would be at another major hotel on Thursday night. Well, I learned a long time ago that in America, unless you can come up with a pet rock idea, write a number one best seller or marry someone that already has it, you do not get something for nothing so, I started asking myself why would this man spend all of that money to fly into Nashville, pay for his sleeping room, pay for the television advertising and pay for the meeting room and do that for me, free. Well, I did not fall of a turnip truck neither did my mama raise a fool, so I went to the book store and purchased every book I could find that had to do with no money down real estate and taught myself and by my own personal experiences, went through the school of hard knocks, so to speak. Do not tell me that you cannot purchase real estate with no money down because I have owned several pieces of property that amounted to over two hundred and fifty thousand dollars ($250,000.00) of value that, I purchased everyone without any money down. This is why I wrote another book of mine that is titled, "Why No Money Down Real Estate Really Does Work,". This book is currently on the market-see Amazon.com, Barns & Noble.com and iUniverse.com.

In America, if you have the drive and ambition then there is only one thing keeping you from becoming wealthy and that is finding the correct vehicle to take you there whether it's construction, real estate, writing a book, or whatever. You just have to find your niche and you may have to try out several different things to achieve your goals. Knowledge is power.

With so many courses available on the internet in this day and time, taking three or four years out of your life to attend school and go out partying every night is simply shooting yourself in the foot.

In this day and time, mothers and fathers seeking to give their children things they did not have are going way beyond what is, in reality, good for the child. For instance, I know of several kids that were given a room, a television, a computer, and their own cell phone. They are allowed to take their food into their room or mother brought their food to their room. They're not given any chores and don't have any responsibility so, is it a wonder that many kids are in their mid to late twenties and are still at home and will not get a job and if, they do get one and realize it is hard work then, they quit because they have not been taught from a child what work ethic is. They are rebellious, self-centered, selfish, and have no respect for their parents whatsoever. When they do not get their way they're just a larger version of what they were when they were a child and throw their temper tantrums but now, they're big enough to destroy their parents' property when they do not get their way.

One could certainly take some lessons in raising children from King Solomon because, God told him that he would be the wisest man who had ever or will ever live and since, he had a lot to say about raising children it just seems to me like a parent should listen to the wisest man that ever lived. Solomon said that "he who spares the rod hates the child". The word "hate" means to love less so if, I have to translate this for you, he is saying if you do not spank your child then, you do not love them. He also said "a child left unto himself brings shame upon his mother" and "he that spares the rod spoils the child". Yes, I realize the argument that many make. I realize because, I am soft-hearted myself and every time I spanked one of my daughters I wanted to sit down and cry but, I had to look past that particular moment and look ten (10) to twenty (20) years down the road to what kind of person they would turn out to be if, they did not learn to respect authority and do it at an early age. Now, my father took it too far. I absolutely got a beating but, there's a lot of difference between that and a spanking. Isn't it strange that a recent article was done on corporate CEO's where, it was found that every one of them, in some form, were spanked when they were children? Want your child to be successful? Give them a spanking when they need it. Do not allow your child to get their way with their temper tantrums. When they get older it will definitely come home to you. If, you are currently having problems with teenagers and they're acting in the way that I have described, then you can only look in the mirror and blame yourself because, you trained them to be the way they are. If, they have no respect towards you, stand up and smart off, curse you, don't get you Christmas cards, birthday cards and such, then you created that child to be the way they are as an adult.

Now, let's get back to where I left off in chapter seven about self-employment and hopefully, I can give you some pointers and maybe open your eyes though, I can not tell you everything because you will have to experience many ups and downs if, you decide to go into business for yourself.

First, I hope I have put enough in this book to show you how the subconscious mind operates and how we listen to the old wives tales about how it takes money to make money, it takes education, you were born on the wrong side of the tracks, and such bologna. Yes, it would be much easier if, you had a little money to start off but, on two occasions, I started with less than four hundred dollars ($400.00) and both times, because of my determination and knowledge that I had acquired, ten (10) years earlier, I became a millionaire.

To show you a little eye opener, being in the construction business, I could go get my nail apron and my paint brush back out and I could probably make two to three times what the normal family income is but, that is only a higher standard of living so, if, I want to become wealthy I can not do it by physically working myself because, there is only so many hours in the day that I can work. There's also the risk I take of getting hurt and being out of employment for quite some time without any income so, the repossession guy would probably give me a visit. The way you become wealthy is being able to duplicate yourself. In other words, get a whole lot of other people working for you and making a little off each one.

I recall several years ago when someone came to my office around lunch time and the secretary was not there. This person sat down in her chair while talking to me. The secretary was doing IRS form 1099 mail outs to people that were subcontractors. I had several branch offices of my business but, I had all of the managers on a sub contract basis and the gentleman that ran my office in Knoxville, Tennessee's 1099 was on the secretaries computer screen and I recall this person being astonished when they saw the screen and called out my managers name and asked me "you mean you paid this guy over one hundred thousand dollars ($100,000.00) this past year?" I replied that I sure did and I would pay him more if, he made me more. The reason I did this was I took something from another self-made millionaire when he said the secret to his success was, he hired the competitions best people and paid them more. You see I didn't care whether he made two hundred thousand dollars ($200,000.00) or three hundred thousand dollars ($300,000.00) a year as long as he made me the same amount. Now, if I have several branch offices doing the same thing, then you can figure out how I made all the money I did.

I encourage you to not share your dream with negative thinking people. They will dump on you with their negative statements, laugh at you, put you down and discourage you from even trying and wind up stealing your dream.

The education world says I can't be a millionaire because I had poor grades, hated school and barely got out of high school. God said, "Ron, oh yes you can and I did. They said I would never make it without some business courses. God said, "Ron, oh yes you can" and I did. They said I was crazy to think I could ever publish a book. God said, "Ron, oh yes you can" and I did. They said I needed a lot of money to get started in business for myself. God said, "Ron, no you don't" and I did it with only four hundred dollars ($400.00) to my name. When I lost everything the first time, they said I was just lucky when I did it the first time and I couldn't do it again with the same amount and no credit. God said, "Ron, oh yes you can" and I did it again. They said I would never own a three hundred and forty eight (348) acre farm with one hundred ten (110) head of cattle. God said, "Ron, oh yes you can" and I did.

The combination of God's help and my willingness to do whatever it took, short of doing something illegal or, immoral is how I did it. I had a desire to succeed so bad, it was almost fanatical. If it took working sixteen (16) hours a day, I did it. If, it took working seven (7) days a week, I did it. If it took giving up some television time, I did it. If you want to be successful in business, those things are a must the first few years until you get it going good. This is America so, if you are going to dream, dream big, dream the impossible. Heck, who knows, I just might meet another hottie that will motivate me and I do it the third time. Maybe this book will make me a millionaire again, who knows?

There is the true story about a boy at age fifteen (15) from California who started a carpet cleaning business while still in high school, doing the work part time. He started with less than one hundred dollars ($100.00) and rented his carpet cleaner at first. While still in school, his business grew so much that his father was able to quit his poor paying job and work full time. After high school, the boy also went full time. He kept paying the price for success by working all the time, eventually got in with insurance companies and handled their water and smoke damage claims and after only three (3) years, was in three (3) states and was listed on the New York stock exchange as, ZZZBEST.

To date, in the past seventeen (17) years, I have only dated one lady. About three (3) years ago, I met a lady named, Linda. Linda and I hit it off the very first time we met. We both had to use the bathroom at the same time so, as we were at the ladies bathroom door, to my surprise, she planted one on me. I have kissed a lot of women but, never had a kiss like that. I started calling her hot lips. Lol. Linda is quite a bit younger than me but, we really didn't notice the age gap as, we had a lot of fun together. She is very beautiful but, mainly, she is a Christian with a heart of gold and a caring and loving heart. We dated about a half dozen times or so but, she was a two hour drive away and I just couldn't manage that every week.

The examples I have given you are just a few of thousands of success stories but, I gave you these to open your eyes to the vast opportunities right in front of you. I hope to have changed your thinking because, in order to change your life, you have to change your thinking. If you ever go into business for yourself, just do the things I talked about and make it happen. Don't listen to gloom and doom thinking people. Stay away from them. Yes, it's a bit scary to go into business for yourself but, a good dose of self confidence will take you a long way. God didn't make a no body and if you think you are then, you are letting others use your mind. I never wanted anyone to give me a thing except a chance but, with only a high school education, no one would so, I made it happen because I never had the thought that I might fail and if I did, I would pick myself back up and go at it again. Only two percent (2%) of all Americans make over one hundred thousand dollars ($100,000.00) a year and I did it twice so, not bad for a dumb ole country boy huh? I just might do it again, who knows?

Feed your mind with good positive things. Read the books I suggested and all you find by someone who has made it in America on their own with little to no money and little to no help. Remember, you are in a free enterprise system in America which means, you can be whatever you want to be and the only thing stopping you is, you. Go make it happen.

I want you to not only feed your mind with positive things, hang around like minded people, I want you to think outside the box, challenge what you have been taught and leave things that will destroy your dream and your body, alone, no matter what others are doing.

Not all but, the typical American male and female work all week then, the highlight of their week is to head to a bar. Ladies, men go to a bar for one reason and it isn't to socialize or, dance. They are looking to get in your pants and they don't care what lies they have to tell you in order to do that. Hey, maybe that's what you want so, let's take a look at what you are really doing. If you smoke, there is about a fifty percent (50%) chance you will get lung cancer and die early. If you drink a lot of hard liquor or, beer, there is a one hundred percent (100%) chance you will die from your liver being eaten up by the alcohol and die young. It is a miserable death. I know, a friend of mine became an alcoholic and died that way. It was a horrible death. Now, liquor is very expensive, it leaves a bad taste in your mouth, it makes people say and do things they wouldn't normally do. Why do you ladies think guys are willing to buy you free drinks? The more you drink, the better his chances of having sex with you. One night, go to a bar, don't drink any alcohol and set back and watch dozens of people make an absolute fool out of themselves. They may be having a good time as they see it but, reality is, they are acting like morons and idiots. Chances are, those drinking will attempt to drive home. What if your drinking causes a wreck and you kill someone's kid? Can you live with that? You will spend a long time in jail for your stupidity. After drinking and partying half the night, next day, you feel like crap, you have a busting headache (hang over). I ask you, is it worth it to drink? Folks, there is nothing but, the devil in that bottle or, can. It's simply not worth it so, don't let the crowd or, friends get you to drinking. It will destroy you as much as any drug or, pill will.

To those who profess to be Christians, I say to you, don't fool yourself, most of you who do drink won't make it to heaven. My best friend kept after me to try a beer and I finally did because I wanted to be a part of the crowd. It's a wonder I am alive today because of all the stupid things I did while drinking. Most want to fight when they get to drinking. Not me, everyone was my friend. Ha I never was a heavy drinker. I may have two (2) or three (3) beers while grilling out and maybe the same in mixed drinks while having a romantic dinner however, every so often, I would drink too much. Just how many times does a Christian have to get drunk to be a drunkard in Gods eyes? Oh sure, you can ask for forgiveness but, when you do then, the next week, you go do it again, I would think that your salvation just might be in danger. No, there is no sin in having a drink but, if you give it up totally, you can be assured you will make heaven. NOTHING is going to keep me from making heaven. One day about eight (8) years ago, I was grilling out on July the 4th and was drinking a beer when, all of a sudden, I get an awful headache. I then started thinking about me drinking and realized every time I had ever done something I shouldn't, I was drinking so, that ended my drinking. I do not need a drink in order to have a good time. I hope you don't either. Always remember, no one wants to put up with and be around someone who is drinking heavy.

I want to talk to you about alcohol for a minute. I realize doing away with alcohol is unrealistic but, if I can get one person to stop drinking or, never drink by what I am about to say, it will be worth my time to type this. Alcohol is too much accepted in our time and culture so, it's not going away. Most drink because it's the social thing to do and especially those in their twenties think they have to drink in order to have a good time. What if I told you it was a proven fact that alcohol was more deadly to you than heroin or, cocaine?

While I am thinking about it, a survey was done to none drinkers by one of the on line companies and they asked to respond in one word what their thought was when they saw someone holding a beer or, other forms of liquor. The most often word answered was, stupid. That's how others see you when you hold a drink of alcohol.

British researchers studied alcohol, heroin, cocaine, ecstasy and marijuana, ranking them on how destructive they are to the individual who takes them and the effect it has on others around them. They also ranked them as to how addictive the drugs were and how they harm the body, its role in breaking up families, friendships and the effect on society when those addicted uses social services and commit crime and go to jail.

Herion, crack cocaine, methamphetamine or, crystal meth were the most destructive to individuals. However, when considering the overall social impact, alcohol, heroin and cocaine out ranked all others. Want to be a dead beat, a no good mate, a no good father, a no good mother, a no good friend and make a fool out of yourself often then, have your way and keep drinking. Do you want people who love you to try and avoid you because they don't want to put up with a drunk? Then, keep drinking. Not only does alcohol have devastating effects on those who drink, it effects those around them. On the average, seven (7) people you know are going to have to put up with you when you make a fool of yourself. When you're drunk, alcohol damages all of your organ systems. It is also tied to a much higher death rate and it causes the drinkers to do things they wouldn't normally do like crime, wife beatings and fornication. Those who drink too much will generally try to drive their car/truck. How would you feel if you killed someone's child or, another person? Many do. Life is hard enough without you shooting your own self in the foot. Don't let others drag you down with them. Now, ladies who care about their skin, let's take a look at the affects of alcohol on your skin.

As with the mind, the body is the same way, what you put in is going to affect what the outside looks like. I challenge you to take a picture of your face then, even if you drink only a couple of drinks, alcoholic drinks, stop for a month then, take another picture of yourself and you will see the difference. Alcohol is known to further the advancement of skin diseases such as, psoriasis and rosacea in some cases.

The most common skin sign of drinking alcohol is, facial flushing. The drinking of alcohol causes the blood vessels in the skin to dilate even if you just drink once in a while. Maybe to your surprise, if you keep drinking, over a period of time, the dilation can become permanent, leading to the formation of spider veins. Permanent dilation can also be caused by the direct affect of drinking to ones liver. Keep on drinking. Not only that but damage to small blood vessels from drinking can cause them to start to leak which allows fluid to enter soft tissue and give a puffy swollen appearance.

Alcohol is known to make you urinate more often so, it actually keeps your body from extracting water from urine in the kidneys therefore, alcohol consumption can easily dehydrate you and can cause dry itchy skin.

Alcohol offers absolutely no nutritional value. Just the opposite, it can and will affect your mineral and vitamin levels by causing a lowering of healthy nutrients that help in carrying oxygen throughout your body and has a special affect on vitamins A, B3 and C levels that are vital in the regeneration of new cells. Keep on drinking.

CHAPTER 8

Overcoming Life's Bad Times

This is now 2013 as I finish this book so, many things have happened over the time period since I last worked on this book in 2007 that, I want to share with you.

About five (5) years ago, my youngest daughter, Rhonda, overdosed on prescription pills. When her sister found her, she was almost dead. I got one of the most shocking phone calls in my life when, her sister, Pamela, called me and told me Rhonda was in the hospital, had overdosed on pills and the doctors said she wouldn't live until morning and if she did, she would be a vegetable. Janie is now my best friend and Rhonda loved her a lot so, I asked her to go with me. It was a three (3) hour drive to Paris, Tennessee. My sister and Janie both knew how much I loved my girls so, they were shocked that I was so cool about it and had told them not to worry, Rhonda would be fine. When I got to the hospital, her doctors told me the same thing about Rhonda being near death. It was an awful site to see Rhonda with a tube stuck down her throat and she looked horrible. I went over to her bed, put my hands on her head and told her I knew she could hear me that, I loved her so much and for her to fight this with all her might and that she would get up in the morning and walk out of the hospital. Next morning, she did indeed get up and walked out of the hospital just fine.

Now, many were praying for Rhonda's recovery so, I am not taking credit for her recovery that stunned her doctors and the hospital staff. God is to receive the glory for curing her when, the doctors and staff thought it was impossible. Now, if you choose to not believe in God, that's your right. Either the trained doctors, the staff and the tests done on her were wrong or, God did cure her. There was no reasonable explanation. I praise God for healing her.

Rhonda married at age sixteen (16). He was a carpet layers helper and never made enough to support my daughter and himself. I was always sending money for light bill and other things. In the early 1990s, I called him one day and asked him if he was good enough to go into business for himself? He said he was but, didn't have the money to get started. At that time, they lived in northeast Arkansas, close to his parents and close to Rhonda's mother. I wanted Rhonda back in Tennessee and she wanted to be here so, one day, I brought Randy to Tennessee, took him to Nashville, Tennessee, went to an equipment supplier and bought Randy all the equipment he needed to get started, gave him an older pick up and let him move in a rental house I had in Clarksville, Tennessee, rent free.

The bible gives us a warning to not deceive ourselves that evil companionship corrupts good morals. Oh, how true that is. Had my best friend not kept after me to try cigarettes, I seriously don't believe I would have ever begun smoking cigarettes, the same with drinking. Lucky for me, though I was never a big drinker, I quit in July of 2006 and haven't drank since. There is nothing but the devil in that can or, bottle. I have seen it destroy so many people and so many relationships. I know no body didn't pour it down her, he didn't force her to smoke pot, do drugs and pills however, she loved him so, when he said, here, try this or that, she did. She got hooked and eventually beat alcohol.

Rhonda had my first grandchild around this time, Morgan. Her brother, Braden was born two or three years later. I spent thousands of dollars on them their whole married life.

Around 1998, I bought a fire damaged home on the lake at Paris, Tennessee and restored it. It was sharp. When Rhonda saw it, she fell in love with it as, it was just down the street from her sister, Pamela. I let them move in rent free again. In spite of that, many Christmases, if it wasn't for me bailing them out, they would have had nothing. I wasn't a fool, I knew where their money was going but, since I had two grand kids I wasn't about to let, be homeless, I kept giving them money and didn't know how to deal with it. Yes, I fussed at them but, neither seemed to have any shame. One was a bad money manager and the other was glad of it, I suppose.

Rhonda was a very affectionate, caring and loving person. She didn't get that from him. Many birthdays, Mother's Days, anniversaries and Christmas Days went by without him getting her a card, much less a present. She was like someone in jail and didn't allow her to go anywhere. She didn't even do the grocery shopping. She became so unhappy that she not only turned to food and gained over one hundred—fifty pounds, she started doing drugs, pills and alcohol. Now, this is the same person who won a beauty contest at age fifteen (15) years old.

Right after Rhonda's recovery, I talked to her seriously about her spiritual standing with God. I told her God had given her a wake—up call, a warning. She still had God in her heart and would attend services just once in a while off and on for several years. About three (3) years ago, Rhonda got breast cancer and it was at a very bad stage. Rhonda went through chemo and radiation treatment and was able to beat breast cancer. Again, I told Rhonda God had given her a second walk up call. She only listen partly though God was on her mind as, she talked with others about him. Not much later, she got bone cancer and went through chemo and radiation treatment a second time. Chemo and radiation treatment must be really difficult as, I have known several strong men who couldn't take it and just quit. Rhonda had an unbelievable will to live. She wanted to see her kids graduate, have kids, etc so bad.

Why am I telling you so much about my daughter, Rhonda? Because on April 11th, 2013, Rhonda died at my home due to bone cancer. I had known for about a year that she was probably going to die. She wanted to come here for about a month and be with me. She was here about two weeks and one day, she laid down to sleep and died in her sleep. I expected her to go back to Arkansas and slowly go downhill from there. She endured unbelievable pain but, to me, she never complained. She put up one heck of a fight to live and borrow time. She had a limp when she walked but, we had a great time and I will always treasure that time together. I am the last one she told that she loved. I am the last one to kiss her good night. I am the last one to hold her. There is always good with the bad I suppose. She had told her mother that she wanted to die in Tennessee so, she got her wish. She died with no pain so, I am so grateful she didn't have to go through the last stages most cancer patients do and suffer so much.

I will never forget Rhonda telling me three things. One, she told me she knew exactly why she got cancer. She said, when God saved her the first time, she didn't listen to his warning and still didn't listen the second time when she got breast cancer. The good is, while she was here, I told her to not dare die on me and leave me wondering if she made it to heaven or, not. She assured me she got things straight with God so, I know where she is at right now. The second thing is, she had this stuffed dog she slept with and it didn't have a name so, I named it bow wow. She had me promise to bury the dog with her and I did. Third, she had me promise her that I would have, "Dads Tooter Toots" put on her tombstone. I took care of her cremation and her mother was to take care of the rest so, I don't know if that got done or, not. If it didn't, Rhonda, this is an everlasting memorial to you—Dads Tooter Toots." I will see you in heaven and NOTHING will keep me from seeing you, mom, dad and many others that I love.

I suppose most of us tend to look down our noses at people who become addicted to alcohol, pills and drugs. One thing I know for sure now, those things don't select ones social standing or, education level. I never did do drugs and pills because I could easily see how they will absolutely destroy anyone who fools with them. This goes back to what I said about the influence others have over you. I know without any doubt that my daughters were raised right and the proper example was set before them. However, the influence others had, including their mate got them to try those things.

After losing Rhonda, I suppose my greatest fear is, losing Pamela before my time to go. Her new husband, Mike and her both have told me she has quit drinking altogether. I hope to God she has quit but, I also wonder if, they just told me what they think I want to hear since I am a six hour drive from them so, it's not easy finding out the truth. Like pills and drugs, I have seen so many marriages and people's lives destroyed by that stuff and I have seen the miserable death that occurs when liquor eats up ones liver. It isn't a pretty scene. Personally, if I ever do marry again, it's hard enough to make a marriage work, much less deal with an alcoholic that daily makes a fool of themselves or, has fooled themselves into thinking it's ok to have a glass of wine at the end of the day. A glass of wine, a can of beer, etc would be just fine however, we all know and those who do that, knows very well that their drinking just one, doesn't always stop there. I will never do anything like drinking to even take a chance that those things will destroy what I want the most in life, my wife. She will be far too precious to me to even take a chance of losing her. If you drink and are married, I beg you for the sake of your family, give it up and that goes with drugs and pills also. How bad do you want to make it to heaven? Face the truth, keep drinking and you won't ever make it.

I know of a couple who tried to mix alcohol, pills, drugs and porn with Christianity. They were upper middle class with four (4) kids, a beautiful home on the lake, a high income, boat, jet skis, nice car and truck. They had it made. I warned them both two years before their lives finally fell apart that they were heading for divorce if they didn't stop what they were doing. I am going to say the same thing to you that I said to them. I told him, "I am telling you, as a husband, if you are doing all God tells you and her, if you are doing all God expects of you as the wife, it's impossible to get a divorce but, if you don't change and do it now, you are heading for a divorce." Sadly, they didn't listen and the ones who really suffered were the kids.

After all I have been through and continue to go through, I am often asked how I handled things without pills, drugs or alcohol. Very simple. I prepared my mind. I filled it with God's word and remembered his promises. When Rhonda died, that just made me more determined that I will not be defeated by Satan and nothing will ever keep me from seeing her again in heaven. In business years ago, I refused to ever quit, no matter what happened. The best way to handle the problems in life is, to get a grip, stop being a wimp, face the problems head on and resolve them, find a solution. Most of the time, our problems are self inflicted because we aren't doing the things we know we should be doing or, we are doing things we know we shouldn't and when we do that, it bites us in the rear. Many people who don't want to face life's problems, run to a doctor, cry and moan that they can't take it and need some pills or, the doctor tells them they are bi polar and need pills. I don't believe a word of it. Life is tough but, remember God said he will not put more on you than you can take. I believe that and I believe drugs, pills and alcohol makes things worse every time.

As I have said if you really want to be happy then, when someone wrongs you, don't carry that around with you on your mind. That's like carrying around an old dead dog chained to your leg. Let it go. Whether they deserve it or, not, totally, completely and immediately forgive them. Do that and hand the problem to Jesus. Now, its his problem and not yours. Another thing I would like to teach you about happiness is, people don't care what you know until they know how much you care. Live by these things and follow Gods instructions to you and you will be so much happier in live and leave the crutches alone, i.e., pills, booze and drugs. Can't you just look around you and see what those things have done to destroy others? Why ever try them?

The bible says, whatsoever a man (or woman) thinks in their mind, so are they. You are what you think about. I have already told you that your mind is like a computer. What you put in it is going to come out. You control everything put in your computer. Yes, there is already available porn but, you control whether you view it or, not. You control every thought that you allow into your mind. You control whether you are going to be sad or, glad. You control whether you will curse or, not. People that are unhappy are refusing to control their minds.

My mom and I were very close and it was very hard on me to all of a sudden, couldn't see my mom again. Holidays were special to her. She passed on October 28, 2012. The way I handled it was, I was so happy for mom, knowing she lived the Christian life. A month later at Thanksgiving, I could have said, oh boo hoo, my momma is gone, so woe is unto me. For the first time in my life, I wasn't going to moms for Thanksgiving dinner. When life changes (and it will), sometimes it may not be pleasant but, we have to adjust and change with it. Thanksgiving morning, I looked at my favorite picture I have of mom, told her how much I loved her and how much I missed her and then, went to a local restaurant and had a great dinner all by myself. Janie was tied up with her family and Pam was in Arkansas so, I made the best of the situation as I could. Had I spent the day filling my mind with sadness, I would have been very selfish and only ruined my day. I was truly happy for mom because I knew she had reunited with my dad and many brothers and sisters who also lived the Christian life. I was grateful to God for allowing all of us to have her for so long and for the good health she had until about the last three months. Even then, we put her in extended care so she was well looked after and not in any pain. I controlled every thought that went into my mind about her.

People, who find dealing with life's problems and don't want to and run to a doctor and get pills to deal with those problems, wear me out with their weak and wimpy attitudes. When Rhonda died, yes, it was much harder on me because of her young age and her unbelievable desire to live to see Morgan graduate. I talked with her also. She was here with me after death, worried about me as, for the first three or four months after she passed, my bedroom door closed every day when, in the previous six years, it had never closed. She still does it.

Sort as an update, over the last several years, I have made pretty good sending out letters to people who have had house fires. In addition to that, in the fall of 2012, another hurricane hit New Orleans. It wasn't too bad, mostly some flooding and shingles off with some interior damage. I went to Gulfport, Mississippi and hooked up with a public adjuster in New Orleans and did his estimating. For those who don't know what a public adjuster is, it's one who represents the homeowner (policy holder), against the insurance company. He paid me on two (2) or three (3) smaller jobs and just over eight thousand dollars ($8,000.00) on a large job. It's been almost a year now and I suppose he is waiting to get paid from the owner however, I didn't agree to wait and his collection problem isn't my problem so, since he still owes me several thousand dollars, I recently had my attorney send him a collection letter.

About the time I went to Gulfport, the VA changed brands on one of my medicines. After about three days of taking the new medicine brand, I broke out in sores all over my arms, back, rear and legs. For some reason, It didn't affect my face. After about three weeks of it not getting better, I went to the closest VA and they switched my medicine back. They also gave me a cream that helped dry the spots. They will eventually all go away but, I still have a few dark brown places where the sores were.

My mom was getting up in years and had lived alone and taken good care of herself but, over about a three month period, she started losing her memory bad and while I was in Gulfport, my sister admitted mom to extended care. After about another week, I just had to go back home and see about my mom as, we were always very close and I loved my mom dearly. At that time, mom was being well taken care of and was able to walk to eat. I had some work to finish so, I went back to Gulfport and that's when I did three big jobs all owned by the same man. Mom was on my mind all the time so, after another two weeks, I went back home for good.

By then, mom's health had really gone down and sometimes, she didn't even know me. She then, got where she couldn't walk and was bed ridden. It was an awful daily sight to watch her die. She passed away on October 28, 2012. Of course, I miss my mom but, I am so happy for her because, without a doubt, I know where my mom is. Though she was my mom, she was one of the most precious persons to ever live. She gave of herself, worked so hard, was faithful to the Lord and had rather someone run over her than to have any unpleasantness. What a special lady and mother.

My little sister is ten (10) years younger than me so, after I moved to Chattanooga in 1970 and she married at age sixteen (16), except for holidays, I hardly ever saw or, talked with her. When I moved to the Nashville area in 1988, that all changed.

After my surgery, I had to make a lot of visits to the doctor and hospital clinics. She came and took me many times. She even bought me one of those really nice and expensive tread mills. That made me cry. However, over the following months, she kept referring to the tread mill as "her" treadmill so, when I lost everything the second time, I let her have it back figuring there must have been a misunderstanding about the treadmill. Since, I have bought my own just like it. She would call me every Sunday morning. After I moved from Nashville in 2006, I seldom heard from her.

As early as 2002, someone kept talking about how this person could pay off this person's credit cards and retire if, this person put mom in a nursing home. This person said this to many family members. Mom, at the time, was in her mid eighties and was in really good health and took care of her home well so, I made it clear that no one was ever going to move my mother out of the home she loved so much unless two doctors told me she was no longer able to take care of herself. This person also made the statement, "If she is depending on me to take care of her, she can forget it," speaking of my mother. Again, this was said to several family members. What a terrible thing to say after all mom did for this person.

When I moved back to my home county and to the country, mom was thrilled to death in spite of me still being thirty (30) minutes away. Every other Friday, I would go get mom and take her to town to have her hair fixed, go to the bank, get groceries and eat out. Believe it or not, mom loved chicken livers rather than a fried breast. Mom was fun to pick on so, we had a really good time together. One day while eating, she asked me if I had time to take her by the bank. I asked her didn't she remember I had already done that? She said her and this person's name was on one regular checking account and that she wanted to take this person's name off, close that account and open one in her name and mine since I was so much closer. I said, "Oh my God Mom, if this person finds out about it, this person will swear I talked you into that. Mom said to not tell this person until after she died.

That didn't work too well. In the fall of 2011, this person, not knowing this person's name was off the account and without mom's permission, tried to take money out of mom's account. How much, I don't know but, made no difference to me as, I came off on them and told them they had betrayed the trust mom had put in them and that their name didn't deserve to be on anything. I had never made any deposit nor taken any of mom's money. I suppose the thought that I may talk mom into taking their name off mom's CD account caused her to panic so for the last year mom was alive, this person came and got mom every other Friday. Until mom just fell apart the last four months of her life, this person and I had not spoken. We had to because of mom's condition. For the first couple of months after being put in extended care, mom could get around fairly well.

About this time, I had an opportunity to go work in New Orleans. I actually stayed in Gulfport, Mississippi and drove to New Orleans a couple of times a week. I had about two thousand three hundred dollars ($2,300.00). I made fairly good but, still haven't been paid several thousand dollars owed to me so, I recently had my attorney send him a collection letter. That's about twelve thousand ($12,000.00) dollars. I have one in Loudon, Tennessee who owes me eight thousand three hundred dollars ($8,300.00) and I have one in Knoxville, Tennessee who owes me about the same. Unfortunately, the legal system wheels turns very slowly so, who knows how long it will be before I finally collect?

I suppose when I told this person that this person's name didn't deserve to be on anything, this person must have panicked so, the very next time mom needed to get her hair done and get groceries, this person drove. I now know why. Eight (8) years ago, when I moved back to my home county, I would take mom to get her hair done, get groceries and take her to the eye doctor when needed since, he was just a few miles away. This person would take mom to Nashville (about an hour's drive from mom's home) when she needed to have a check up and would always go back to the exam room with mom and the doctor because mom wouldn't always tell the doctor all she had told this person so, this person heard everything the doctor told mom.

To my surprise, this person announced to me that this person had been given a power of attorney by mom. Mom and I were very close so, I knew she wouldn't do that without talking to me first so, I started checking behind this person. I found out this person had gotten the power of attorney on October 28, 2011, just three (3) months after taking over getting mom every other week. Mom was age 94 at the time and died a year to the date in 2012.I later obtained mom's doctor records and found out this person very well knew that mom had a bad case of dementia and was not mentally capable to give this person the power of attorney. I got mom's condition from her doctor records that stated this, five (5) months before this person got the power of attorney.

On February, 10th, 2012, this person used the power of attorney on mine and mom's account at Regions Bank and withdrew three thousand dollars ($3,000.00) from mom's account without mine or, mom's permission. The branch manager told me he is the one who handed this person cash. At the same time, to keep me or, mom from finding out this person got the money, this person had the monthly bank statements changed from mom's address to this person's daughters address in another town in Tennessee. I found all this out because I didn't trust this person and I would check on the balance from time to time. I thought I would let this person know I wasn't quite as stupid as this person may think so, I sent this person an e-mail about the same time, asking this person if the three thousand dollars ($3,000.00), was a loan. I never got a reply.

I forgave this person but, I am still angry at her for taking advantage of an elderly woman, my mom. One of the worst things this person did was, mom had depended on this person to help get Christmas and birthday presents. Mom could still get around amazingly at age ninety four (94) however, she would get worn out if she walked a lot. On the Christmas following me catching this person trying to take money out of mom's account, this person made sure I didn't get anything for Christmas from mom nor, a card or present for my birthday three (3) days after Christmas. I am a big boy so no big deal other than I saw just how mean this person can be. Mom never had any idea and I never told her. It was my last Christmas with mom. It was for mom that I wanted to sit down and cry for after this person took advantage of mom's mental condition just so this person could have some revenge against me. Heck, I wasn't the one who tried to take money from mom's account without her permission so, what right did this person have to get upset at me?

A week before mom passed, it was obvious she was going to die very soon. This person sprang into action once again. I had been going to check on mom's house often and so, one trip, I wanted to re-read moms will but, the will and all of mom's financial paperwork was gone. This person, without the permission of me or, the other heirs, had taken all of them home with this person.

This person went to Regions back, used this person's illegally gotten power of attorney, closed mine and mom's account, transferred the same money to a new account. The day after mom passed away, this person started using this estate account as this person's own, writing one check to eat out, made four (4) of this person's own credit card bill payments and even made the electric and water payments the whole eight months at mom's house while someone else paid no rent and me and the other heirs got stuck with three fourths (3/4) of the electrical and water bill while someone else paid nothing yet, had a job.

This is a person I trusted and so did mom. I trusted this person, plus, this person "claimed" to be a Christian. This person reminds me of what Jesus had to say in Revelation chapter 3: 14-21 about the church at Laodicia. He was talking about them "playing church" with one foot in and one foot out. In modern day terms, he told them to make up their minds to either get all the way in or, all the way out that the way they were going, made him sick at his stomach. Sounds like a modern day hypocrite. I will add you people who run around talking about God or, Jesus all the time, I have learned to stay away from you because the life you actually live, tells a different story and you do so much damage to the Church because your life runs others off and you also make me sick to my stomach. Money doesn't spend well in hell.

After all the money numbers were sent to the proper authorities in order to settle the estate, I refused to sign off because, one, the figures were wrong. This person had that the starting balance was a little over two thousand when, in fact, this person had spent over twenty four thousand dollars ($24,000.00) out of mom's CD account which was fine as long as this person accounted to the court, to the proper authorities, to myself and the other heirs but, this person had not accounted to anyone. I had borrowed seven hundred dollars ($750.00) and this person had overspent mom's personal account by over three hundred dollars ($300.00) and neither of those was listed.

The main thing about this person's numbers was, this person had told me she was going to charge a fee of one thousand five hundred dollars ($1,500.00) for all the gas and time this person has spent going through mom's things. I explained to this person that this person was trying to charge the estate time and gas for going through this person's own things since I had given this person my half of the contents, trying to avoid any arguments over money. The last thing mom would have wanted. That's equal to me trying to charge the estate for going to mom's to get my own tools out of her out building.

I hired an attorney. This person responded by hiring an attorney. Remember this person's one thousand five hundred dollar ($1,500.00) fee? This person now submits a new list with mileage charge of over three thousand two hundred dollars ($3,200.00) based on a mileage allowance chart off the IRS web site. Problem with that was, mileage deduction is for a business, a charity or, business moving miles and it clearly said so at the top of that page. This person swore under oath that this person spent over 200 hours "cleaning" when the truth is, this person was sorting through this person's own property, having yard sales and having individual buyers come there to buy some things. In fact, someone very knowledgable told me she didn't clean anything as this person claimed it was cleaning to prepare the house for sale.

The end result was, this person didn't get a thing for any fees and this person spent out more in attorney fees which I am guessing at three thousand dollars ($3,000.00). My attorney was a Christian friend who only charged me very little.

Why did I tell you all this? Because, part of the settlement was, this person wanted me to agree there would be no further contact between us. That would kill mom but, suited me fine. Oh, sure, I forgive this person but, sometimes, we have relationships where the other person just keeps on doing things to hurt you and though you may wish that person the best, wish they would repent and change their ways, you stay away from that person so, that person doesn't have another chance to hurt you. Besides, such drama is known to harm ones health. This person has everyone in my family so upset at this person that they don't want to see this person or, talk to this person again because of this person's evil ways and how this person did others over a few dollars.

All that aside, this is not the end of my book, just the beginning. I am starting a new business and everyone will know my name. Who knows, maybe I will get me a hottie to motivate me. Ha. A pretty face and a hot bod will motivate a man one hundred percent (100%) of the time. Lol

While writing this book, several have asked what happened between me and Janie that we got an annulment? The annulment was instead of a divorce because we weren't ever really married. Janie is my best friend so, just let me say, she thinks it's my fault and I know it was hers. We have debated it for twelve years now and still won't agree on that or, our religious views in another twelve years so, the best for us is, to not discuss either. ha We think the world of each other but, we can't live in the same house together. There is no sex because we are both Christians and don't care to go to hell over committing fornication.

In closing, I want to say, if I have helped just one person have a better and happier life or, helped give courage to someone dying to be in business for themselves then, it will be worth the time it took to tell the story about my life. Don't miss heaven. Obey God and get your home there as your reward. I know I am. Good luck to all

ABOUT THE AUTHOR

Mr. Searcy is the author of "How Anyone Can Understand the Bible", "Divorced At The Courthouse But Not In Heaven" and "Why No Money Down Real Estate Really Does Work", all currently on the market with, "From Bankruptcy To A Millionaire-Twice-A True Story" now on the market that you are reading with, "Why God Didn't Make Anyone Homosexual" to follow next.

BIOGRAPHY/AUTOBIOGRAPHY/MEMOIR

Ron Searcy is a seasoned author, having published, "Divorce At The Court House But Not In Heaven", How Anyone Can Understand the Bible", "Why No Money Down Real Estate Really Does Work" and now, the incredible story of his life an how, twice, starting with only $400.00 both times, became a made millionaire. The things that happened to him during tho years and he over came them all is, almost unbelievable. In h next book, "Why God Didnt Make Anyone Homosexual" he w write the most eye opening religious material of out time. He hopes to publish that book in 2014.

Mr. Searcy feels that anyone can acomplish what he did and obtain wealth. This book is about a man kids made fun of because he didnt do good in school but, without doing anythi immoral or, illegal, showed if one has the desire and is willing pay the price, almost anyone can do what he did, all without college degree.

U.S. $12.95

ISBN 978-1-4917-297
51
9 781491 729762

iUniverse®
www.iuniverse.com

aved, Single, and Satisfied

Vickie Blakeney Mitchell